Y0-BQN-998

FAMILY AND SOCIAL CHANGE
IN AN AFRICAN CITY

NORTHWESTERN UNIVERSITY African Studies

Number Eight

FAMILY AND SOCIAL CHANGE
IN AN AFRICAN CITY

A Study of Rehousing
in Lagos

Peter Marris

Northwestern University Press
1962

© *Institute of Community Studies 1961*

Library of Congress Catalog Card Number: 62–8927

Printed in Great Britain

CONTENTS

ACKNOWLEDGEMENTS

THIS study was financed by a grant to the Institute of Community Studies from the Leverhulme Trust. The Joseph Rowntree Charitable Trust met the expenses of a preliminary visit to Africa, when I was preparing the enquiry. The Lagos Executive Development Board and Professor Barback of the Nigerian Institute of Social and Economic Research encouraged me to undertake the study in Lagos: J. C. Henderson, the Chief Executive Officer, and the staff of the L.E.D.B. provided many services on which the study depended. They continued to be just as helpful after it became clear that some of my conclusions were unacceptable to them.

Samuel Akinadewo, my assistant research officer, and L. G. Ajayi, Chairman of the Central Lagos Residents' Association, interpreted the interviews, and added valuable notes and comments on them. Gilbert Dopemu helped to organise the survey work. Peter Lloyd, Alison Izzett, Mrs. Winifred McEwen and Jean Herskovits gave me much advice and information while I was in Nigeria, and read the book in draft. Dr. Otto Koenigsberger encouraged me to believe that the conclusions of a sociologist could be worth something to architects and town planners, and Professor Daryll Forde that they might not be contemptible to anthropologists.

I received very useful comments on this book in draft from Mrs. Prudence Smith and Professor Richard Titmuss; from members of the Institute of Community Studies Advisory Committee—Dr. John Bowlby, Sir Alexander Carr-Saunders, Euan Cooper-Willis, Geoffrey Gorer, Robin Huws Jones, Professor Charles Madge, J. L. Peterson, Peter Townsend, Lewis Waddilove and William Wallace; and from my colleagues at the Institute. The map and diagram were drawn by Colin Mackenzie and Michael Smith.

To all these, and to the people of Lagos whom I interviewed, I am very grateful; I hope the result seems to them to justify their help and encouragement.

PETER MARRIS

Bethnal Green,
March 1961.

INTRODUCTION

EVERY morning, dense files of cars and bicycles, lorries and buses, edge across Denton Causeway and Carter Bridge into Lagos Island. The office worker from the mainland rises at six to fight his way into an overcrowded bus, which, after an hour's journey, disgorges him ten minutes late with the lame excuse of another go-slow. A street plan which served a town of thirty thousand, travelling on foot, is now overwhelmed by the tenfold crowd of clerks, administrators, shoppers and traders who struggle to their work on wheels. But it is not only for their sake that the centre of Lagos is under pressure to rebuild. With the approach of independence, the people of Nigeria began to look more critically at their Federal capital, and saw in its congested lanes of ramshackle houses a poor reflection of their aspirations. As the Minister of Lagos Affairs remarked, 'it is the mirror through which foreigners make their initial appraisal of Nigeria and many regard it as an index of the progress and prosperity of Nigeria.' The condition of central Lagos, he said, was 'humiliating to any person with a sense of national pride.'[1]

Certainly the visitor who explores the rambling footways behind the department stores and office blocks, will see much that is squalid. He must pick his way amongst rams and chickens rummaging in the garbage, as he seeks a dry foothold beside the open drains. The houses on either side are for the most part of one storey, with here and there a gabled attic thrusting out of the red-brown sheeting of the roof. Inside there may be anything from three to a dozen rooms, or more—some so piled with beds and baggage that there is hardly room to set a chair.

But the visitor will also notice the vitality of these overcrowded lanes. Since quarters are so cramped, families do little but sleep,

[1] In a debate in the House of Representatives on 13th March, 1958.

make love, and store their belongings within doors. For the rest, they cook, eat, gossip and carry on the business of their lives in their back yard or in the street. A group of children squat on a porch, while their Arabic teacher takes them through a verse of the Koran; a woman plaits her neighbour's hair; in the late afternoon, men carry their game of draughts or table tennis into the lane; and on a Thursday or a Saturday night, the street may be filled from end to end by a wedding or a funeral party, sipping their beer and whisky under a shelter of matting. In the back yards, carpenters and millers, printers and blacksmiths run their workshops. On the verandahs, tailors bend over their machines. Signboards advertise building contractors, football pool agents, wireless repairers, importers. And in every yard and doorway and verandah, from booths and shops, or hawking up and down the lanes, women are trading—in cottons, velvets, muslin, damasks from Lancashire, Madras, Japan; enamel-ware from Hong Kong; incense from Bombay; dried stockfish from Norway; cigarettes, tinned foods, cola nuts; fruit and vegetables brought by canoe across the lagoon; fried plaintains for office workers and bowls of porridge for dockers from the waterside. Here, in this jostling, shabby, busy neighbourhood, a way of life has taken roots.

In the interests of redevelopment, the people of this neighbourhood are now being prised from their familiar setting. As Nigeria becomes a sovereign nation, its Federal capital is at the centre of the social and economic pressures shaping a new society. New hotels and office blocks, banks, parliament buildings, roads and bridges transformed the townscape on the eve of independence, and this spectacular renewal in glass and concrete is an expression of the urgency with which material progress is demanded. But the intricate relationships of a settled community are notoriously difficult to transplant. Slum clearance, by the sudden changes it thrusts upon these relationships, forces the pace of social evolution. When streets and houses are pulled down, the way of life they were built to contain is also called in question. How will the people of Lagos adjust their way of life to match the new image of Nigeria which its capital is striving to reflect?

2

The newly emerging nations of Africa are probably the most rapidly and radically changing societies in the world. In less than a hundred years, they have developed from self-sufficient communities of farmers into countries with a sophisticated constitution and administration, modern cities, industries, a money economy, a written culture, and an educational system based on the knowledge and values of the highly developed industrial empires which until recently governed them. They are impatiently seeking to achieve equality with these richer nations. To succeed, they need not only capital and technical advice, but knowledge of the society they want to develop. Without this knowledge, serious social problems will arise which might have been mitigated, especially in the fast growing urban centres where change is most rapid. Yet until recently, there have been few studies of African metropolitan life. There is least systematic knowledge of society, just where the most urgent and far reaching decisions about its development are being made.

This book explores some of these changes in the capital city of the largest of the new African states. It is based on an enquiry into the family relationships and means of livelihood of the people of central Lagos, and the way in which slum clearance affected them. I decided to relate the study of change to an examination of the Lagos slum clearance scheme, partly because a previous study by the Institute[1] had discussed the effects of slum clearance on family life in London, and some of its conclusions might be relevant in the context of African city planning; but more especially because although the Lagos scheme only bears on a minority of the city's population, it illustrates very concretely the implications of social change. The design of a house, the layout of a street, mould social behaviour, and influence very directly the way in which people live. They interpret in terms of physical space the ideals by which planners believe social relationships should be formed. Housing policy is therefore much influenced by the most articulate values of society. On a new housing estate, private life is framed within the provisions

[1] Reported in *Family and Kinship in East London* by Michael Young and Peter Willmott, 1957.

of public policy. At the same time, latent changes in social structure become manifest in reaction to new surroundings.

In presenting this study, I have tried to keep in mind also more immediately practical problems. While the study was being planned, the Lagos Executive Development Board—the public body responsible for the Lagos scheme—invited me to include in the scope of the enquiry a question which particularly concerned them: how could the petty traders and small shopkeepers so common in central Lagos be provided for when the neighbourhood was redeveloped, without destroying the dignity and amenity of a modern commercial centre? Some possible solutions are discussed in the course of chapter nine, but such a question cannot really be answered in isolation from the complex of social and economic life. I have tried to show how, for instance, patterns of marriage are relevant to the trading of women, and how marital relationships are in turn moulded by traditions of family life, which themselves play an important part in determining the structure of economic affairs. Against this background, particular problems merge into more fundamental aspects of society. To the administrator, looking for a practicable solution to an immediate difficulty, the results of an enquiry such as this may seem disappointingly imprecise. But social research cannot finally determine issues of policy which may depend as much upon the funds and staff available, and the political position of the government of the day, as upon the findings of the research. Nor can it decide conflicts of value and interests. It can only reveal the nature of the situation in which a solution must be found, and suggest the likely consequence of different policies.

I have interpreted the findings of the enquiry to throw new light especially on two aspects of change: the social problems facing tropical town planners and governments urging forward a policy of very rapid development; and the pressures of a radically changing social structure upon family life. But to understand how slum clearance embodies ideals and reinforces pressures which are re-shaping the social order, we need to look back to the origins of Lagos, and the traditional structure of the family, as a starting point from which to trace the direction of change. So the first half of the book describes how the people of central Lagos have adapted their customs to the common experience of city life. Only some aspects of family organization most directly relevant to the theme are examined in any detail— the patterns of residence and association, the mutual help exchanged between kin, and the way in which husbands and wives conceive their responsibilities in the affairs of the household. I have tried to show how the loyalties of kinship maintain themselves in a metropolitan setting, and how this affects relationships in marriage, and the emotional attachments in which children learn to place their trust. A more comprehensive analysis of family structure would have been beyond the scope of the present enquiry. (In describing family relationships I have used the terms most familiar to an English-speaking reader. A specialised terminology would have tended to obscure the similarities between family life in Lagos and an English city, and its greater precision is not essential to the argument, since particular relationships are not analysed in detail.)

The slum clearance scheme and its consequences are discussed in the latter half of the book. The final chapter considers more broadly the way in which, as I believe, divergent trends in family life may be radically affecting the class structure of society.

3

The enquiry is based upon four different sets of interviews carried out between August 1958 and September 1959. The most important of these are two comparative studies of householders in central Lagos and on a rehousing estate in the suburbs, where families have been resettled when their homes in central Lagos were pulled down. A further group of householders were interviewed in a block of streets on the mainland of Lagos by my research assistant, Samuel Akinadewo, after I had left Lagos. I have referred to this sample in one or two places in the text, to illustrate living conditions outside the slum clearance area. Finally, a sample of individuals resident in central Lagos was drawn from a census compiled by the Lagos Executive Development Board, to complement the information from householders by statistical data from a larger area.

The rehousing estate sample of householders

On the rehousing estate, a random sample of one in fifteen

addresses was selected from the record of tenancies held by the L.E.D.B. The houses are for the most part occupied by one household only, but all the households at the addresses drawn were investigated. Two thirds of the heads of households interviewed were men, most of them married, and under fifty. Nearly half the women, however, were widowed, and mostly passed middle age.

The central Lagos sample of householders

It was much more difficult to frame a sample in central Lagos. The houses are much larger and contain many households: the only list of occupants—the census compiled by the L.E.D.B. to assess rehousing needs—is not altogether accurate. Nor does it distinguish how the residents are grouped in households: it records only the name, age and sex, and whether owner, relative of the owner, or tenant. A household is in any case very puzzling to define. People who share the same room may be unrelated, and live entirely independent lives: on the other hand, a wife may live several streets away from her husband, and yet cook for him every day, and depend on him for support. So it seemed best to choose a group of streets at the heart of the clearance area, and interview all the households living there, treating as one household those who lived under the same roof, 'ate from the same pot', and kept house together. This had the advantage that returning day by day to the same neighbourhood, I could observe more of its life for myself, and know the people better: but the representativeness of the sample is more open to question. Three quarters of the heads of households interviewed were men, and as on the rehousing estate, while most of the men were married, half the women were widowed or divorced, and tended to be older. This follows from the nature of the samples, since a woman living with her husband could only in unusual circumstances be considered the head of her household.

The central Lagos sample of adults

Since the households in central Lagos could not be selected at random from the slum clearance area, these interviews were complemented by another sample drawn from the L.E.D.B.'s census. Every tenth person over twenty years old was selected from the lists they had compiled, covering several of the areas into which the slum clearance programme had been sub-divided. A team of interviewers was recruited, and briefly trained to use a questionnaire which covered, in more precisely tabulated form, the same topics as my own interviews. As would be expected, the proportions of men and women in this sample are more nearly equal, and there is much less difference between the sexes in age and marital status than in the samples of householders.

The mainland sample of householders

The questionnaire for the central Lagos sample of adults was also used to interview the heads of households in a block of houses in Ebute Metta. The neighbourhood seems typical of the back streets of Ebute Metta and Yaba, but it is difficult to know how far it is representative. Here nearly all the household heads were men, a third of them single, and much younger than the householders affected by slum clearance. They were comparative newcomers to the city.

In the time available for the study, only small samples could be drawn. Eventually, about 20,000 people will be affected by the slum clearance scheme, and six thousand had already been moved when this study was made, Roughly half of these were then living in the rehousing estate. The population of Lagos itself is approaching 400,000. The samples are only about 3% of all the households to be affected by slum clearance, and of those living on the rehousing estate, and about the same proportion of all adults in central Lagos. The numbers in each group are as follows:

		Interviewed	Refused	Not contacted
Householders:	central Lagos	110	2	2
	rehousing estate	63	1	1
	Ebute Metta	132	–	–
Adults:	central Lagos	372	7	103

The rate of refusal is so low because the people of Lagos are naturally courteous to strangers, and because they hoped the enquiry might help them, and were concerned to put their point of view. Even so, they answered with much patience questions that must often have seemed tedious or irrelevant. Amongst those who could not be contacted, seventy-five had left for another address, nineteen could not be traced, five were away, six had died, and one proved to be a baby a few months old.

The composition of the samples, together with other statistical findings of the study are summarised more fully in Appendix I. Only a few tables have been included in the text, so as not to interrupt the thread of the discussion by too many detailed figures. To illustrate the argument, I have used where possible quotations from informants who spoke English. Most of the interviews on the rehousing estate were in English, and in central Lagos, thirty-two of the interviews with householders were entirely in English, and eleven in a mixture of Yoruba and English. The rest were nearly all in Yoruba. I was lucky enough to have the services of two Yoruba speakers, Mr. L. G. Ajayi, the Chairman of the Residents' Association, as well as Mr. Akinadewo, my research assistant, so that when we were together my assistant concentrated on recording answers verbatim in Yoruba while Mr. Ajayi interpreted. Translations from Yoruba in the text are noted. Appendix II describes in more detail the methods of the enquiry, and the questions asked.

These four samples do not provide a very tidy or substantial basis for a sociological study, but the research worker in an African city has to some extent to choose between refinement of technique and a less systematic search for insight into the society he is studying. The population is so varied that some kind of sampling is necessary if the results are to be at all representative. But there is no ready-made frame of reference from which to draw a random sample, such as the electoral register provides in Britain. Probably the most reliable method is to draw a grid over a plan of the town, and sample the squares. However, when the town is densely populated, each square is likely to include a large number of people to interview, and further selection is difficult. To carry out such a plan, a team of interviewers must be thoroughly trained and carefully supervised. A survey of this kind would have taken all the time and resources available for the Lagos study, without going deeply into the topics with which it was most concerned. It seemed better to concentrate on fewer, more discursive interviews, which I could undertake myself, and risk the assumption that they were typical. I do not think the people I interviewed can be very different from others affected by the slum clearance scheme. How far their way of life is characteristic of Lagos as a whole, and represents a characteristic pattern of African urban life, I hope future investigators will explore.

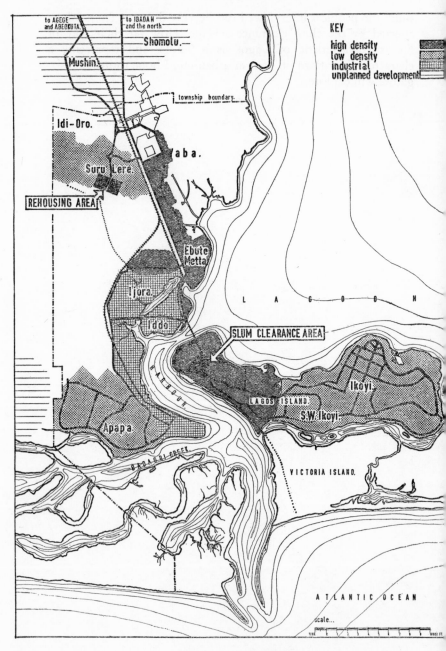

Sketch map of Lagos

I

LAGOS

As you drive into Lagos from the airport, the town
reaches out to meet you—an estate of green and terra-
cotta flats for business executives; a cluster of speculative
lodging houses, raw and perfunctory, thrown up in an acre of
tree stumps; a furniture factory. Already at Mushin, seven miles
from the centre, you are enclosed in the urban area. Petrol
tankers, buses and high-stacked lorries, lurching precariously,
heave their way along the highroad between untidy ranks of
concrete houses. Beyond are the older suburbs of Yaba and
Ebute Metta. Here, to the left, the grid of streets peters out at the
shores of the lagoon in unmade roads, timber yards, and trade
houses where rents are high and accommodation mean. To the
right, across the railway line, lie the new estates of the Lagos
Executive Development Board—neat lines of modern bungalows
marching out into the bush.

At the southern end of Ebute Metta, by a market and the
Mainland Hotel, one road curves off round the western shore of
the lagoon to Apapa, the deep water harbour and industrial
estate. Behind the warehouses and acres of oil storage tanks, the
mainly expatriate residents of a new suburb struggle to impose
lawns and flower beds on a waste of sand. Skirting the oil tanks
on the other side, a sandy track leads to the boundary with the
Western Region, where several acres of mud or bamboo-walled
dwellings have spread out beyond the reach of the building
regulations of the township.

The other road from Ebute Metta leads over the Denton
Causeway to Iddo Island—the railway terminus and starting
point for cross country buses—and so across the two thousand
foot span of Carter Bridge to Lagos Island itself. This is the heart
of the city, and its oldest quarter. The streets here do not bear
the names of former Governors of the Colony, or towns of the

I

Protectorate: they commemorate noble families and the powerful merchants of the slave trading days—Chief Taiwo; Balogun, a warrior who became a Lagos trader; Kosoko, the rebellious king, who choked the lagoon with the corpses of his enemies; or Madame Tinubu, a wealthy trader, and his rival's niece, who harassed a succession of British consuls by her intrigues. Department stores and Government offices, banks and consulates rise above winding lanes which you will find marked on maps of eighty years ago. Here, too, are the great open markets of Lagos; the oldest churches and mosques in exhausted Gothic and fairground oriental; the faded roccoco of 'Brazilian' houses. Along the southern shore of the island runs the Marina, a promenade designed by the first acting Governor of Lagos, who was determined to have, 'at least one decent walk'. It leads past the Governor's residence towards the race-course, the Prime Minister's office and the Supreme Court. Here the island is crossed by a canal. Beyond it lies the garden suburb of Ikoyi, with its golf-course and European club. It covers twice the area of the rest of Lagos Island, and houses about one-tenth the population.

Here a creek separates the island from a sandy spit of coast. Along the beach, fishermen haul their nets, Sunday crowds splash cautiously in the breakers, and the white-robed prophets of a Christian sect toll their hand-bells in palm-fronded pens. Behind them rises a new luxury hotel. By it will be the parliament buildings of independent Nigeria, flats for the elected members, and across the reclaimed swamps will spread another estate of villas for the capital's elite. So Lagos will have completed its progress to the sea.

The whole urban area extends about ten miles from the eastern end of Lagos Island to the outskirts of Apapa, and about twelve miles from the site of the new parliament to Mushin. It contains a continually growing population which by 1960 approached 400,000, about two thirds of them Yoruba. But as a port, a great commercial centre and capital city, it draws people from all over Nigeria. And as it grows outwards, branching across creeks and swamps, so its centre is pressed upwards storey by storey, thrusting out of a congested pack of rust-red iron roofs. The city is bursting out of the confining waters which protected its beginnings.

Lagos

THE HISTORY OF LAGOS

The earliest inhabitants of Lagos were hunters and fishermen. They settled first on the smaller of two swampy, low-lying islands, which straddled a neck of the lagoon between the mainland and a sandy spit of coast. Here they found good fishing and a natural defence. The winding channels of the lagoon led westward to the Kingdom of Dahomey, and eastward to Benin. To the south, across a shallow bar, the waters of the lagoon flowed into the sea—the only breach in the coastline for a hundred miles in either direction. To the north lay the expanding Yoruba empire of Oyo, a loose affiliation of city states, from which these early settlers originally stemmed. But the Lagos settlement was isolated by swamps and forests from the heartland of this empire, whose capital city lay two hundred miles distant in the upland plains. About three hundred years ago, Lagos became tributary to the powerful kingdom of Benin.

It may have been the remnants of a Benin Army, taking refuge in Lagos after a defeat, who brought it under the subjection of their king.[1] But though Lagos continued to acknowledge the sovereignty of Benin until the middle of the last century, it remained a predominantly Yoruba settlement. According to legend, a Yoruba chief had originally divided Lagos amongst his sons, whose descendants, the White Cap chiefs, held the residual rights to all the land of the two islands. The Yoruba kings appointed by Benin to rule in Lagos did not usurp these traditional rights, and land was held by the families who settled in Lagos according to Yoruba custom.

[1] The early history of Lagos is obscure. There are differing Yoruba, Benin, and Ijaw legends. My account is based chiefly on A. C. Burns' *History of Nigeria* and the first volume of *The Peoples of Southern Nigeria* by P. Amoury Talbot. Talbot suggests that the Lagos area was under the domination of Benin before 1472, when the first Portugese explorer arrived, and that it was reconquered by Benin about 1660. But the names and circumstances of the second invasion are so similar to the first, that it seems more likely that he has mistaken two versions of the same event for two invasions. In Burns' account there was only one conquest. His genealogy of the Kings of Lagos would date the accession of Ashipa, the first Oba appointed by Benin, at about the beginning of the eighteenth century. G. B. A. Coker, in *Family Property Amongst the Yorubas* writes, 'In or about 1790, the Oba of Benin from the Southwest of Nigeria invaded and conquered Lagos' (p. 186). But this is surely too late a date, since only thirty years later Richard Lander could record that, 'Lagos is and has been from time immemorial, tributary to the powerful King of Benin'. See also J. B. O. Losi, *History of Lagos* and J. B. Wood, *Historical Notices of Lagos*, written in 1877.

3

A small settlement in a coastal swamp was not of much consequence to the kingdoms of the hinterland. But to the merchant
fleets of the Portuguese, Lagos afforded a useful harbour in
their search for a sea route to India. The first Portuguese explorer
reached the coast of southern Nigeria in 1472, and by 1500,
Portuguese merchantmen had begun to frequent Lagos harbour.
The King of Benin landed there on his return from a visit to
Portugal in 1550. Forty years later, the first Englishman called
there—James Welsh, in the *Richard of Arundell*, on an expedition
to Benin.

But the Portuguese trade soon declined. After the Reformation,
the Papal bull granting the Portuguese a monopoly of the West
African trade was no longer respected, and they met increasing
competition from the Dutch and English. The rivers of this part
of the coast were, besides, dangerous to navigate, and valuable
cargos scarce. A contemporary account remarks, 'there is nothing
to be had in them, but a little quantity of Elephants teeth; so the
labour to fetch it is not worth the paines, by means of the dangers
that a man incurreth by entering the rivers, by reason of sands'.[1]
The Lagos bar remained a serious obstacle to trade for another
three hundred years.

By the beginning of the eighteenth century, mercantile interest
in gold, ivory, cotton, wool or tailed pepper had been diverted
to the growing demand for slaves to work the plantations of the
New World. By 1730, seventy thousand slaves were shipped
annually from the West African coast: in 1771, one hundred and
ninety-two slave ships left England, fitted up for nearly fifty
thousand slaves: at the end of the century, two hundred thousand
slaves a year were being transported across the Atlantic. The towns
along the creeks and lagoons from Lagos westward to Wida made
fortunes by the slave trade, and lost them to their predatory
rivals. Wida, Appa, Porto Novo, Badagri, became by turns the
greatest slave markets, fought each other, and were overrun.

Lagos, at the end of the eighteenth century, was beginning to
grow prosperous on this international trade. Captain John
Adams, who called at Lagos in 1789, observed, 'An active traffic
in slaves was carried on at this place, particularly after Ardrah
was deserted by the French traders. It has always been the policy
of the Lagos people . . . to be themselves traders and not brokers.

[1] Quoted in Talbot from a Dutch source. p. 80.

They therefore go in their canoes to Ardrah and Badagri, and to the towns situated at the north eastern extremity of Cradoo lake, where they purchase slaves, Jaboo cloth, and such articles as are required for domestic consumption'. His description of the furniture in the Oba of Lagos' palace suggests the useful articles and handsome rubbish that the people of Lagos acquired by this trade . . . 'There were tumbled together, promiscuously, articles of trade and costly presents, in a state of dilapidation; namely, rolls of tobacco, boxes of pipes, cases of gin, ankers of brandy, pieces of cloth, of Indian and European manufacture, iron bars, earthenware, a beautiful hand organ, the bellows of which were burst; two elegant chairs of state, having rich crimson damask covers, all in tatters; a handsome sedan chair without a bottom and two expensive sofas without legs.'[1]

But Lagos was still, at this time, a port of secondary importance, partly because it charged heavy dues to slave ships: Captain Adams estimated its population at only about five thousand. The most flourishing centre of slave dealing was at Badagri, forty miles to the west along the creeks. It was, however, much more vulnerable than Lagos to the depradation of its rivals.

From the end of the eighteenth century, the Yoruba empire began to disintegrate. The Fulani were pressing on its northern boundary, and the Kingdom of Dahomey from the west. The old capital, Oyo, lost its ascendancy, and the city states of the empire ravaged each other in an internecine struggle that lasted until the intervention of the British. The slave trade not only encouraged this warfare, but upset the balance of power: the southern Yoruba towns and villages had earlier access to European guns and ammunition, and could block the trade routes to the north. Lagos began to attract refugees from the mainland: here they were protected from slave raiders, and could themselves share in the growing slave trade of the island, whose natural defences protected it from the attacks of rival towns.

But trade with the interior was still a risky, if profitable, undertaking—especially since, 'it has always been the policy of the Lagos people to be themselves traders and not brokers'. A distinguished member of the Moslem community described to me how his father, who must have settled in Lagos about 1840,

---

[1] Captain John Adams, *Remarks on the Country extending from Cape Palmas to the River Congo*, pp. 96 and 101.

used to travel to Ilorin with cotton and tobacco, which he bartered there for slaves. The journey could only be made deviously, at first by canoe along the creeks and rivers, and then on foot at night, travelling from village to village through the bush with the help of a local guide. Sometimes they might be held up for weeks or months, when local wars made it too dangerous to proceed. The distance is less than two hundred miles, but he was sometimes away for years at a time, returning at last with slaves and horses, which he sold to the people of Dahomey. The great canoes used in this traffic can still be seen plying Badagri creeks, lashed to a motor launch and piled high with baskets and vegetables.

The newcomer to Lagos at this time could easily acquire, at the cost of presents of gin and cola nuts, permission from the owning families to settle on unoccupied land. As yet only the rising ground at the west of the main island, where the palace stood, was densely built. The rest of the island, apart from a few farms, was bush. The town itself was built of mud and thatch, fouled by refuse and plagued by water-rats—or so, at least, it seemed to European eyes, dimmed by continual fever and dysentery.

But by the middle of the nineteenth century, a new kind of immigrant had reached Lagos—the repatriated slaves, many of whose houses still grace the older streets of Lagos. They built of brick, the walls plastered and washed with white or ochre, the doors and windows enlivened with plaster mouldings. Most of them were of Yoruba origin, returning from the plantations of the New World. Others came from Freetown, where those rescued from the slave ships were first resettled. Many made their way inland, but some used their knowledge of the world to start in Lagos an international trade. They settled at first in a quarter on the low ground between the foreshore and the hill, which became known as Olowogbo—'he who asks for his money back'—from their practice of selling on credit, and asking for payment later. Some of them were at first themselves slave dealers.

The great expansion of Lagos came, however, not from the slave trade, but its suppression. In 1807 the British Government passed an act prohibiting, from the first of March of the following year, the carrying of slaves in a British ship, or their landing in a British colony. A British naval squadron was formed to patrol

the West African coast, and it intercepted, between 1829 and
1849, over a thousand slave ships. But at the end of this period,
the export of slaves was as great as it had been fifty years earlier,
before the Acts—some 85,000 people a year. It became clear that
the slave trade could only be destroyed at source. British officers
approached the King of Dahomey, but though he was courteous
and sympathetic, he could not see his way to abandoning the
trade in default of an alternative revenue. So they turned their
attention to Lagos, where a struggle for the succession to the
Obaship offered a chance of diplomatic intervention.

In 1841, the King of Lagos was blown up in an accidental
explosion of gunpowder, and was succeeded by his uncle Akitoye.
His claim was disputed by his nephew Kosoko, who had found
himself passed over for a second time. Four years later Akitoye
made a rash gesture of conciliation, and invited his nephew to
return to Lagos. Kosoko promptly raised an insurrection: he
exterminated his uncle's family and supporters to the number of
about two thousand, while Akitoye himself fled to Badagri.
Here the British took him under their protection. Since Kosoko
himself would not discuss the abolition of the slave trade, Consul
Beecroft and the local officer of the British squadron decided to
restore Akitoye by force. An attack in November, 1851, was
abortive: a more determined assault on Boxing Day also failed
to carry the town, partly because the European slave traders had
given valuable advice on the defences. The following day the
town was set ablaze by gunfire from the ships in the river, and
on the 28th Kosoko fled. On New Year's day 1852, Akitoye
signed a treaty promising to abolish slave-trading, human
sacrifice, and the execution of prisoners of war, and to open
Lagos to missionaries and legitimate trade. At the end of the
same month, Her Majesty's Government wrote complaining that
Consul Beecroft had no business to attack Lagos, and was
exceeding his instructions.

Akitoye's treaty was naturally unpopular with the principal
traders of the town, and he died of poison in the following year.
His son Dosunmu succeeded him, with British support, but his
position was precarious. The slave-trading interests were against
him, and Kosoko was continually plotting to recapture the town,
where he still enjoyed strong support. In view of continual
unrest, and Dosunmu's inability or unwillingness to enforce the

terms of the treaty, the British authorities decided to bring Lagos under their direct control. In 1861, Dosunmu was obliged to sign a treaty ceding Lagos to Britain, and surrendering his authority over its thirty thousand inhabitants. In exchange, he was to receive a pension of two thousand pounds a year.

With the establishment of Lagos Colony, the present town began to take shape. The thin line of European buildings—missions, merchant's homes, the Governor's residence, warehouses—began to expand along the foreshore, screening the congested African town. The missions built churches and schools; trading firms built depots for the growing export of palm oil; and Government provided institutions of public order—a police court and a prison.

But development suffered from the shallow and at times unnavigable bar, the continual warfare that blocked the trade routes to the interior, and the deadly climate.

All European descriptions of Lagos in the nineteenth century harp wearily on squalor and disease. Sir Richard Burton, appointed consul to the Bight of Biafra, regarded his appointment with robust defiance: 'They are trying to kill me, but I shall live, just to spite them'. He considered Lagos, 'certainly one of the most unhealthy spots on these malarious shores', and its site 'detestable'. He recommended street widening, drainage and public health regulations, and a beginning, at least, was made with a promenade along the foreshore. But at the end of the century, the death rate amongst the European population was worse than ever. A grim item in the *Lagos Standard* protested that, 'it was time that something should be done to relieve the grave diggers from the strain of work to which they are continually subjected'—they were working a twelve-hour day, Sundays included. Drainage and swamp reclamation, scavenging and fresh wells, seemed to make little difference: the grave diggers were still overworked.

For these reasons, in spite of expanding trade, Lagos at first grew relatively slowly. In 1862, the revenue of the Colony—which included Badagri and some smaller towns on the lagoon—amounted to about seven thousand pounds, and exports, almost entirely palm oil, to sixty thousand. By 1890 the revenue was over fifty thousand, and the value of exports exceeded half a million. But the population of Lagos had increased by only about seven thousand in these thirty years: the census of 1891 returned a figure of 32,508.

However, in the next twenty years the population more than doubled. The protracted civil war between the Yoruba states, which had handicapped trade with the interior, was finally brought to an end in 1893 through the intervention of the governor of the colony. The way was at last clear for regular communication with the hinterland. By 1900, a railway was running as far as Ibadan. The line ran from Iddo, the smaller of the two islands of Lagos, across a road and rail bridge to the mainland. A second bridge two thousand feet long was built to connect Iddo with Lagos Island, over which there ran at this time a steam tramway. By now, too, the causes of malaria were understood, and the colonial administrator stood a better chance of surviving his appointment. A European quarter was established at Ikoyi, in the deserted eastern half of the island, where it was hoped the risk of infection might be less. Roads were metalled, electric light installed, canals cut and swamps drained. Finally, in 1905, work was undertaken to remove the last handicap to the development of the city. Moles were built at the entrance of the habour, and the channel dredged. By 1914, Lagos had become established as the principal port of Nigeria.

At the same time, its political importance grew. The government of the colony had become independent of the Gold Coast in 1886, but its direct responsibility was limited to Lagos and a few towns on the shores of the lagoon. In 1906, however, the administration of the colony was amalgamated with the Protectorate of Southern Nigeria, and in 1914, with Northern Nigeria. Since then Lagos has remained the centre of the political life of the country: by 1921, its population had already reached a hundred thousand, and it was to reach over a quarter of a million before it finally became the federal capital of independent Nigeria.

Like so many cities, thrust into importance by the accidents of history, the features to which it owes its development are now its most tiresome limitations. The earliest settlers were, no doubt, attracted by its isolation, and it survived as a centre of the slave trade because the waters of the lagoon protected it from attack. As the refugees from civil war, and later the repatriates from Freetown and Brazil came to make their homes around the original settlement, the centre of the town grew into a densely packed and unplanned quarter, without roads or sanitation, where families had long-established rights. Commercial houses, administrative offices, hospitals and government quarters grew up around this quarter, and from it communications in every direction have to be funnelled through a series of bridges and causeways—to the new deep water habour at Apapa, to the airport, to the suburbs, to Nigeria. A site which suited a canoe only frustrates a Cadillac, and the whole town clamours with protesting motor-horns.

THE ORIGINS OF SLUM CLEARANCE

Although energetic governors had undertaken drainage, swamp reclamation and road building since the turn of the century, an instrument for effective planning of the township was not created until 1928. In that year, the Lagos Town Planning Ordinance set up a Board, to be called the Lagos Executive Development Board, with authority to order the demolition of insanitary buildings, and to carry out town planning schemes 'with the general object of securing proper sanitary conditions, amenity and convenience in connection with the laying out and use of the land . . . within the township area of Lagos'. The Board was made responsible to the Governor, and included representatives of public services, the Town Council, the Lagos Chamber of Commerce, and the public, under the chairmanship of the Commissioner of the Colony. When the post of Commissioner—later re-designated Chief Administrative Officer, Lagos—was abolished in 1958, Sir Kofo Abayomi was appointed to the chairmanship by the Federal Minister of Lagos Affairs, to whom the Board is now responsible.

The work of the Board started with a small executive staff, a grant of £200,000, and promise of further funds when these were exhausted. A few years earlier, bubonic plague had broken out in parts of the island, and between 1925 and 1928 there were several serious epidemics. The Board's first major undertaking, therefore, was to clear one of the areas worst affected. An officer of the L.E.D.B. recalls how at that time every day when he drove down the road to his office, he used to see the white flags up over the houses where the victims lay. By 1930 work was under way, but soon after the revenue of the colonial government was seriously hit by the world-wide depression, and no further funds were available; staff was cut, and expenditure retrenched. However, by 1939 the L.E.D.B. had cleared fifty acres on the north shore of the Island, and drained an insanitary swamp—Reclamation Road, where the L.E.D.B. now has its office, runs through the area. The original owners, many of them fishermen, were compensated at market values, but no alternative accommodation was provided for them. They were offered the opportunity to repurchase plots after clearance, paying off the cost of the land over several years, but few did so. Concrete houses of two or three stories, with clumsy balconies above the shop fronts, now file down the straight streets.

The war interrupted further work, and the staff disbanded. After the war, concern with slum clearance revived, but met with opposition from the owners of property to be affected. In 1955, however, the L.E.D.B. embarked upon a scheme to redevelop seventy acres of central Lagos, involving about two hundred thousand people, to be phased over five to seven years. From the inception of the scheme, independence for Nigeria was in prospect, and the determination with which it was carried through was inspired as much by the position Lagos would uphold as the federal capital, as by the obvious overcrowding and lack of sanitation in the area. All the same, the working out of the plan ran into difficult social problems. To understand how these difficulties arose, it is necessary to understand the way of life of the people of central Lagos, and how the patterns of their social and economic life are interrelated.

2

THE GROUPING OF FAMILY
RELATIONSHIPS

SINCE Lagos was originally a Yoruba town, the way of life
of its longest-settled quarters derives from Yoruba traditions. In the old established neighbourhood at the Western
end of Lagos Island, over 90% of the people are Yoruba. East-
wards across the island, the proportion of Yoruba drops to
76%, while at Ikoyi it is only 30%. In the same way, as the
suburbs spread outwards over the mainland, the population
becomes more mixed. The proportion of residents born in the
township falls, and the number of Yoruba declines from 83%
in Ebute Metta to just over 50% in Yaba and Apapa: the remainder are predominantly Ibo. But apart from Ikoyi—the home
of senior civil servants and business executives with their
domestic staff—the Yoruba account for over half the population
in every ward of the town, and they are three-quarters of all
the residents of Lagos.

In the four streets of central Lagos which I investigated, four-
fifths of the households were Yoruba. But before describing
their family relationships, a preliminary account of the traditional
pattern of the Yoruba family may help to show more clearly how
customs have yielded or adapted to urban life.[1]

THE TRADITIONAL YORUBA FAMILY

The Yoruba have always been town-dwellers. They clustered
together in settlements of everything from a few thousand to
hundreds of thousands, around which was thrown a mud wall
about eight feet high. Each family would have its permanent home
within the walls, farming land in the surrounding countryside.
At the busiest seasons, the workers might stay for a while

[1] The structure of traditional Ibo society is briefly referred to on page 40.

12

at a temporary farm house, but the family compound within the town remained their headquarters. By analogy, people from other parts of Yorubaland sometimes say, 'Lagos is only a farm to us', meaning that they have come to make money, and hope to return to their home towns, when they have harvested their fortune.

Each of the family compounds in the traditional Yoruba town housed a lineage, or part of a lineage, tracing its descent from the same male ancestor. The rooms would be arranged round four sides of a courtyard, with a single gateway. Opposite the gate were the private room and parlour of the most senior member of the family, while his married children, his brothers with their wives and children, and any other relatives and dependents would occupy the rooms on either side: there might be quarters for strangers by the gate. Each adult member, including the wives, had their own room, the young children sleeping with their mothers, or on the verandah which surrounded the courtyard.[1]

But every lineage will tend, generation by generation, to outgrow its compound. Where there is no space to extend the original buildings, adding new courtyards, part of the lineage must establish a new home elsewhere in the town. If the offshoot can find a site nearby, it may remain subordinate to the parent branch, but the further it moves, the more likely it is to become an independent social unit. In this way, new segments form themselves. Each will recognise the same founder, who is commonly represented as having established himself in the town at the time of its origin, and trace their descent through his children. These descent groups were the basic units in the political structure of the town: they lived together, acknowledging the authority of their most senior member, and were represented as a group in the affairs of the community.

---

[1] Nowadays, the traditional design tends to be modified: the well-to-do put up two-storey houses of a more European pattern, faced with concrete and decorated with balconies. Modern examples of compounds are common only in the remoter towns of Yorubaland. Peter Lloyd gives an example from Shaki—a house built for himself by the Onishaki in 1951. It has twenty-seven rooms, arranged round a yard about a hundred foot square. 'In it reside not only his own children but also the children of his late elder brother and some more distant kinsmen. Each adult man and woman has a separate room, young children sleep with their parents. The children of Popoola (the Onishaki) and those of his brother live on opposite sides of the courtyard, those people who are more distantly related live near the entrance. Thus all the inhabitants of the courtyard trace their descent from a common ancestor.' P. C. Lloyd, "The Yoruba Lineage", p. 237.

The members of the compound are not, however, a single economic unit. Each married man, with his wives and un-married children, and any other kin—such as his widowed mother or a young unmarried brother—for whom he was responsible, would form a separate household. He would farm his own allocation of the family land, and his own household would cater for themselves. When a man had many wives, and so could spend little time with each, they and their children be-came virtually subsidiary households on their own, the children of the same mother being drawn together by close ties of loyalty and affection.

Thus the smallest social unit in the Yoruba pattern of kinship is the mother and her children. They form part of her husband's household, to which, also, others of his dependents may be attached. Several such households live together in the rooms of a compound, recognising the most senior man as their head. These lineages belong, in turn, to a more comprehensive lineage which, as it has grown, has branched into segments, each living in one or more separate dwellings. Finally, the whole lineage itself is part of a vaguer social grouping, whose members recog-nise a distant kinship with each other, though the relationship is not directly traced.

Through his membership of a lineage a man acquired land to farm, a place to live, and representation in the affairs of the community. Titles, offices in religious cults, and—traditionally—distinguishing facial scars, totems and taboos are also passed down through the lineages. In most affairs, the group of relatives living together in the same compound and recognising one head, is the predominant social unit: within it, the household is subordinate. This emphasis is reflected in the words used to describe them.[1] All the men of the family of the father's genera-tion are commonly called 'father', all women 'mother': nephews and nieces are 'child', cousins 'brother'.

To particularise the relationship of individuals, a phrase must be used—'my elder brother's male child', 'my mother's junior sister'. Within the broad classification of relatives by generation, the differences most emphasised in language are those of seniority. There is, for instance, no single Yoruba word for brother or

[1] See William B. Schwab, "The terminology of Kinship and Marriage among the Yoruba".

14

sister, nor for sibling: the elementary terms are *egbon* for an elder sibling and *aburo* for a junior. This is because status within the family group, and in society as a whole, is largely determined by seniority, and one of the most important functions of terms of address is to express these grades of authority. In general, seniority is determined by age and generation, but where these conflict with each other, or with qualities such as wealth or education which lend a man exceptional prestige, the kinship terms tend to be modified to reflect recognised status. Thus, an uncle younger than oneself will not be called 'father', and a younger cousin of outstanding achievement will be senior, rather than junior, brother. The kinship group, besides its other functions, is therefore also a hierarchy of status, which determines the social position of its members.

Women marry into their husband's families, and live with him in a compound of his lineage. Their status within his family is determined, not by their age, but from the time of their marriage to him. They are junior to all members of his family already born. A wife should not, for instance, presume to call a young child of her husband's family—even his child by another wife—by its personal name. She must invent a nickname for it—'velvet bottom' (*ibadi aran*) or 'slender one' (*opelenge*). Nor may she exercise authority over it, if it was born before her marriage. In principle, all members of his family junior to her husband are also 'husband' to her—since traditionally, one amongst them would inherit her as wife were she left a widow. This term of address is used to women as well as men, since a widow might be nominally 'married' to her late husband's sister if no suitable man was available to care for her. But as a man may not inherit either wife or property from his juniors, a woman addresses her husband's seniors as 'father' or 'mother', not 'husband', since marriage with them is out of the question. Thus, for a wife too, her particular relationship with her husband is merged into a wider relationship with his kin. In the language of family address, she becomes wife or child of his whole compound.[1]

---

[1] In the discussions of family relationships which follow, I have used the English terms in their usual sense, not as translations of Yoruba words. This follows the practice of Yoruba themselves when they write in English, and avoids confusion. Although this ignores differences between Engish and Yoruba in the classification of relationships, these differences would only be important to a more comprehensive analysis of Yoruba kinship than is here attempted.

But marriage does not deprive a woman of her rights within her own family. A daughter shares an equal right with sons to inherit use of her father's land and family house. In practice, she would not formerly have had much reason to exercise these rights: once married, her home was with her husband, and he and his family supported her from the produce of their own land. Her children belonged to his lineage. There was farm land to spare, and to sell a family house was considered disgraceful, so neither had any commercial value: besides, no individual had any right to claim a share of these assets. They were owned by the family as a whole, not jointly by its members, and each had only a right of use. However, in the southern towns of Yorubaland, a man might claim land to farm from his mother's side as freely as from his father's side, and would make his home with members of his mother's or his father's lineage accordingly. In this sense, Yoruba society has never been exclusively patrilineal, at least in Ondo, Ijebu and amongst the Egba.

However, the most characteristic pattern of residence amongst the Yoruba has been a group of the sons and grandsons of the man who established their common dwelling, with their wives, children and dependants. Marriages, funerals, disputes, the upkeep of their home, the care of the sick and infirm, the education of children, and the place of its members in the community were the concern of the whole group. It recognised the authority of a single head, the status of each member within it being defined by his seniority. The terms used for family relationships emphasise, in the same way, the predominance of the group over the individual, merging particular relationships in broader categories.

This conception of family life has, of course, become less coherent and universal over the past hundred years. People travel more widely for work and education, they have acquired private wealth in cash, built houses in a western style for their personal use, and sought prestige outside the hierarchy of their lineage. The individual, by his vote, and his access to courts of law, now stands in an immediate relationship to civic authority, no longer formally protected and controlled by the family to which he belongs. Yet the traditional concept of the family still has a profound influence.

16

The Grouping of Family Relationships

The family life of central Lagos has grown out of this tradition, though it has changed more radically and more swiftly than elsewhere in the Yoruba country. At the time of this study, there were still several large compounds in central Lagos which had been occupied by the same family for several generations. One, for instance, had thirty-eight rooms, another nineteen, both of one storey and built round a courtyard, in which was dug a now disused well. None of the houses included in the study conformed so closely to this characteristic Yoruba plan. But one was the home of a family extending over three generations of households, each with its own room, very much as in a traditional compound.

This house was built by a wealthy trader about a hundred years ago. It fronted on to a narrow lane, the walls patched with corrugated iron, the windows boarded with cream and black shutters, grimed with age. Inside the door on the right, a passage extended past two rooms to an open yard, where chickens and guinea fowls clattered in their pens. A second passage facing the entrance led past three more rooms to a larger yard at the back of the house, where the households cooked, washed and kept their stores. Sheds lined two sides of the yard, and lavatories were built into a corner. Inside the passage a narrow staircase gave access to the upper floor: the three lower steps were of concrete, the remainder thin wooden salts, worn away by years of use. At the head of the stairs was a landing with a gable window, where in the rainy season basins were spread to catch the leaks. On either side were sets of rooms, low-pitched under the iron sheeting of the roof. The walls and ceilings were of uneven, cream-painted boarding, and there was a gap between wall and floor, through which appeared the supporting poles of the eaves. On this floor were six more rooms, beside two small ante-rooms through which they were reached. Altogether, the house contained eleven rooms, each occupied by a separate household.

As with many of the old houses of Lagos, it seemed shabby and neglected. The furniture of each room was bare and functional—a bed, a few wooden stools or folding chairs, a cupboard, a pile of trunks and boxes, mats thrown on the floor. In the passage

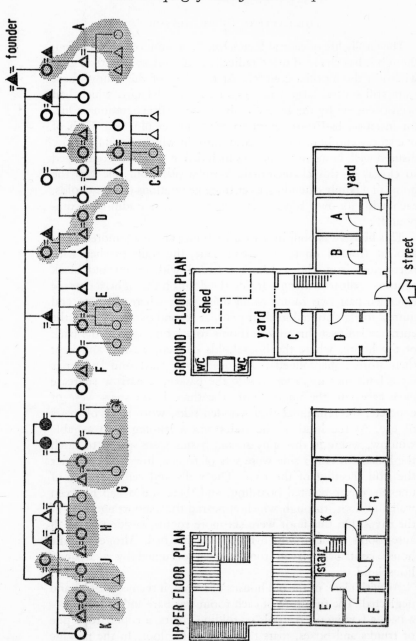

Family relationships of the occupants of a house in central Lagos. Letters indicate the rooms occupied by each household. Children are shown on the kinship chart by symbols in fine line, adults by heavy line.

hung a mirror and a wall clock, no longer working. The only decorations were the calendars of commercial firms—the playfully exotic landscapes with which airlines like to match the months, or Coca Cola girls with their insatiable thirsts—and large wall almanacs put out by Lagos publishers, with inset photographs of chiefs and leading politicians. But in spite of their apparent indifference to appearances, the family was deeply attached to their home.

The most senior member of the house, a vigorous woman in her seventies, was the only surviving child of the original owner. She spent most of her day in a corner of the passage which flanked the front of the building, where every visitor would pause to pay her their respects. Here she presided over the affairs of the house. She shared a room and parlour with her eldest son, his wife and the wife's twelve-year-old niece, who helped with the housework. Two other rooms were occupied by women of her generation; the widow of one of her brothers, with her daughter and grandchild, and the widow of a half brother with three grandchildren. Most of the rest of the house was taken up by six of her nephews, with their wives and children, and usually one or two young girls of the wives' families. Lastly, one room was used by the grand-daughter of one of her brothers, who was separated from her husband. In all, these ten households contained eighteen men and women, and sixteen children. The head of each was a child (or his widow), grandchild or great-grandchild of the original owner of the house. In this sense, they lived as a traditional Yoruba family. But there were many other grandsons and great-grandsons who, because of their work, or simply because there was no place for them, lived elsewhere, either with other relatives or in rooms they had rented.

But there seem now to be relatively few houses in Lagos owned in common by a family, and entirely occupied by them, though such houses are still usual in other Yoruba towns. In the first place, the growing scarcity of land on the Island, and the needs of Government and expatriate commercial firms, have modified the customary tenure of land and housing. This customary law does not recognise individual titles; land belongs to the family which occupies it, for as long as they and their descendants require it. They may allow an outsider to make use of it, in return for a proportion of its yield, but they may not sell it, nor can any individual member dispose of his rights in it at will. If he does not wish to exercise his right to live or farm his share of property himself, the family as a whole will decide to whom it shall go. Ultimately, rights revert to the lineage, and from the lineage to the chief. Until a hundred years ago or so, all land in Lagos was held under the same customary law.

Shortly before the British occupation, however, the King of Lagos began to make individual grants of land. Though he may have exceeded his rights in this, these grants were confirmed as crown grants, when Lagos became a colony. So already, a hundred years ago, something approaching individual freehold titles were becoming established. The owner could, therefore, dispose of his property as he chose, and because land was in demand, the buying and selling of property became accepted practice. Family property, too, came on the market, the profit being divided amongst the members of the family who shared its use; though even in such cases, where the purchaser acquired an individual title, courts have generally accepted that his descendants inherited the property in common, according to traditional practice.[1]

This has meant that though there is much family property in Lagos, owned in common, it does not remain indefinitely within the family, nor is it exclusively occupied by them. Since there is no room to expand, the children and grandchildren of the original owner outgrow their inheritance, and are forced to find a home elsewhere. They may eventually decide to sell it, each realising his share of its value, or let it out to tenants.

Most old property has by now been broken up into smaller dwellings of two to half a dozen rooms, each opening into a passage, or a yard at the back of the house to which the passage leads. These houses are usually divided amongst several un-related households, each occupying one or two rooms, and between 60% and 70% of the residents are tenants. Once tenants are established, they can only be evicted by a slow and expensive

[1] See G. B. A. Coker, *Family Property amongst the Yorubas*, particularly for his account of the interpretation of customary law in Lagos. His discussion is based on cases heard in High Courts and Magistrates' Courts. P. C. Lloyd gives an account based on decisions of the Native Courts in 'Some Notes on the Yoruba rules of succession and on "Family Property" '. Outside Lagos, Native Court decisions are a better guide to prevailing practice under customary law. There are no Native Courts in Lagos.

process of law, and the courts, aware of the pressure on accommodation in Lagos, will not allow them to be exploited or left homeless. A family cannot therefore easily expand even in its own property, unless it has complete possession. The overcrowding of Lagos tends increasingly to frustrate the development of a traditional extended family.

A man with many children and dependants, even if he were wealthy, would find it difficult now to establish a permanent home for his descendants in central Lagos. For instance, a prosperous flour importer bought, a few years ago, a house of ten rooms. To gain possession he had to evict twenty tenants: two applications to the courts failed, and he was only successful at the third attempt because they did not appear to state their case. This household amounted in all to eleven adults and sixteen children, crowded together in five rooms with a large hall. One of these rooms served as an office, and the hall was often stacked high with merchandise. In the evening, the sacks were pushed to one side, and the young children took lessons together: at night they spread their mats on the floor.

Apart from his two wives and sixteen of his children, he lived with his mother, a sister, two of the sister's children, two grown sons of his mother's sister, two young cousins, and three nieces. They all ate together, catered for by his senior wife, and depended upon him for support. The young children were with him for the sake of their education: the cousins, he explained, 'belong to my father's side. They were brought to me for teaching; their father is helpless, and they want them to go to school.' The father of the nieces was in Government Service, 'and transferring up and down the country, the children didn't get a proper education'. The sons of his aunt helped with his business: one had been an English tailor—'but Lagos has changed to native dress, so there's not much for him to do. He helps me a bit'; the other, 'wants to do a bit of trade in sand and the like. He calls himself a contractor. But they are bonded to me. I give them board money just to live on'. Finally, his sister had joined him at his special request. 'I begged leave of her husband for her to stay here to look after my mother, as she cannot see, and I wouldn't like to bring a stranger into the house to lead her about, and know her secret.'

Such a household might in time, as the children grow up and

marry, develop into an extended family sharing in common their father's property. Already one married daughter was living independently in another room of the house. But the five other rooms were occupied by tenants of long standing. So the owner's children will probably have to buy or rent their own accommodation, and if rooms in their father's house eventually fall vacant, they may prefer to rent them out again, since they will by then be established elsewhere. Once property is fragmented, and tenants have acquired rights, a family can no longer expand from generation to generation in the same place.

For these reasons, there were only four houses in the four streets investigated in the present study exclusively occupied by the family which owned them, and two of these only contained a single household. Thirteen other houses were shared between members of the owning family and their tenants. Six of these seventeen homes had been bought by one of the present occupants, and although the remainder had been inherited from father or mother, grandfather or grandmother, usually only a few members of the family which shared its ownership actually lived there. The twelve other houses in the streets were entirely let out in lodgings.

These twenty-nine houses contained from one to eleven rooms, two-thirds of them with half a dozen rooms or less. Some were of brick with ornamental plaster work, some of weather boards or corrugated iron, one so old that it had sunk below the level of the ground. One house contained a printing press, another a mill where the local housewives brought pepper to be ground, and pieces of stockfish to be carved on the circular saw: a large shed on the corner housed a private shool. But the rest of the buildings was all used as living space: and from their overcrowded rooms, the households overflowed into the street. Unsurfaced, dusty or flooded according to the season, the lanes were impassible to traffic, and the residents could spread themselves at leisure. One of the lanes had been blocked off years ago—to prevent thieves, so it was said, from making their escape that way. At its far end, every evening, a young clerk, a store-keeper and a dealer in religious books dragged out their chairs round an endless tournament of draughts. The oldest resident, her hands stained indigo by years of dyeing, sat by her doorstep in an easy chair; the dyeing vats were embedded in a corner of the lane under a shelter of matting. The young wives would drop her a curtsy as they passed to and fro, baskets of trade goods piled on their heads. Higher up the lane, the wives with young babies gossiped and joked. Here the eldest of a family of nine set her clients' hair, under the eye of her formidable grandmother, who kept a whip on her bed and boasted that she was not afraid to use it. Beyond the narrow alley which gave access to the lane, some of the women set out bread and fried dough-cakes for sale.

Within these twenty-nine houses, 110 households occupied 151 rooms—labourers sharing one cramped, dark lodging with two or three others; prosperous merchants enjoying the luxury of a parlour; craftsmen with their cabinets, bicycle parts or dismantled radios stacked in a corner. Three-quarters of the heads of these households were men, nearly all married: the women householders, however, included roughly equal numbers of married and widowed, with a few divorced. Almost 40% of all these households comprised only a man and his wife or wives, with their unmarried children. In 6%, husbands and wives lived by themselves; in another 7%, there were only father or mother and unmarried children, and 7% were men and women on their own. The rest included married children, grandchildren or other relatives. So, though these households were made up of very varied relationships, the majority were small, and only about a third included others apart from parents, children and grand-children. The family group, therefore, no longer as a rule shares a common home, and the households live apart.

Even where these households are small, however, the members usually have relatives nearby. They have lived so long in the neighbourhood that family connections have ramified in the surrounding streets. In the sample of household heads, nine-tenths of the resident owners had been born in Lagos, more than half of them in the house where they still lived. Two-thirds of all their brothers and sisters lived within a few minutes walk of them on Lagos Island, and the same proportion of their children over the age of sixteen. And though many had lost their parents, five-sixths of the mothers still surviving lived as near. Three-quarters of them shared their house with at least six other adult members of their family—3% with upwards of sixteen relatives. They were not, therefore, isolated from their kin.

The tenants had naturally not lived so long in Lagos, and had settled more recently in their present homes. Table I compares owners and tenants in the sample of householders.[1]

TABLE I

LENGTH OF RESIDENCE

	In Lagos			In present house		
	Owners	Tenants	All	Owners	Tenants	All
10 years or less	—	16%	11%	12%	58%	45%
11–20 years	3%	30%	21%	3%	17%	13%
21 years or more	9%	37%	30%	27%	24%	24%
Born there	88%	17%	38%	58%	1%	18%
Total %	100%	100%	100%	100%	100%	100%
Number	33	77	110	33	77	110

Nearly a third of the tenants had been born over a hundred miles from Lagos, in other regions of Nigeria—especially Yoruba from the district of Ilorin, with a few Hausa and Nupe from further north, and Ibo from the east. Most came from the Yoruba towns of the Western Region—Abeokuta, Ibadan, Awe, Ijebu Ode, Ondo. Though they expected to spend their working lives in Lagos, they still maintained close ties with the branch of their family in their home town, where they might hope eventually to retire. They came to Lagos to earn a wage, or profit from a trade, leaving their farm land to other members of their family: and brothers and sisters who, like themselves, had gone out into the world, did not necessarily follow them to Lagos. So they had proportionately many fewer relatives both with them and near them, and in contrast with the resident owners, scarcely any of

[1] The percentages for the larger sample of 372 men and women show the same trends. The widest discrepancy is in the proportion born in Lagos: the figure for owners—88%—is the same, but 30% of tenants, and 54% of all the larger sample were born in the town.

them had more than five other adult members of their family in the same house.

The tenants were not, however, a population of transient strangers: 60% of the household heads, and over 70% of the larger sample had lived in their present home for at least six years. As time went by, and rooms fell vacant, they tended to gather other members of their family round them. Table II shows that amongst the sample of householders, while the relationships of the owners were always closer, about half or more of the tenants lived near to relatives of their own generation.

TABLE II

HOUSEHOLDERS WITH RELATIVES LIVING
WITHIN A MILE

Percentage of household heads* living within a mile of:	Owners % (100%=)	Tenants % (100%=)	Total % (100%=)
A Parent	83% (18)	27% (49)	54% (67)
Husband or wife's parent	61% (18)	35% (55)	41% (73)
A brother or sister	75% (24)	61% (67)	65% (91)
A half brother or sister	90% (20)	49% (55)	59% (75)
Husband or wife's brother or sister	72% (25)	57% (65)	61% (90)

* Excluding those with no parent, brother or sister, etc. living

The table suggests how tenants gradually extend their family relationships in the neighbourhood. Two-thirds of them had left their parents at their home town when they came to Lagos. Since some have married men or women from Lagos families, a rather higher proportion live near parents-in-law. They are closest to their own brothers and sisters: over a third had a brother or sister in the same house—an elder brother who had provided for them when they first arrived, a younger sister who might find a husband amongst their Lagos friends, a younger brother finishing his education, or looking for his first job. The difference between owners and tenants is least of all in their relationship with their grown children. 65% of owner's children over sixteen years of age lived within a mile, and 54% of the tenant's children.

The fullness and integration of social life in central Lagos derives chiefly from its Yoruba population, who are either born or long settled there, and whose family connections have grown round them. Most of them had brothers or sisters and grown children living no further than a short walk away, and though the figures are lower for the older generation, there is still a higher proportion of old people than elsewhere in the city. The immigrants from more distant parts of Nigeria had fewer ties in Lagos and felt less at home there. Some of the northerners interviewed—who accounted for 7% of the householders—seemed little integrated with Lagos life. Three traders from Kano, who rented the rooms of one small house, had been living in Lagos for seventeen to thirty years, yet none of them could speak either English or Yoruba at all fluently: nor, apart from their wives and unmarried children, had they any relatives in Lagos. The few easterners interviewed also complained of their isolation from their kin. A young dispatch clerk who had not been home for five years said, 'I've no special interest in Lagos. I'd prefer my own land if I could get a job there.' An Ibo cook to a Lebanese family, who had worked in Lagos since 1932, complained, 'I am eight years without knowledge of my country, I am hungry to go, but when all time I spend here, how I get money to go home?' However, these non-Yoruba immigrants from the Northern and Eastern Region, and occasionally from Ghana or Sierra Leone, do not settle in large numbers in the centre of the town, and they amounted to only 11% of the householders interviewed. The recent immigrants, who swell the younger age groups, can seldom find rooms in this long settled quarter, unless another member of their family is already established there.

The stability of central Lagos stands out in contrast to the mainland, where many of the houses were originally built for letting. For comparison, 132 householders were interviewed in a block of trade houses in Ebute Metta, built at the end of a road running from the highway to the shores of the lagoon. They were mostly younger men, recently established in the city. Ninety per cent were tenants, and less than half of them had lived in Lagos for more than ten years. Two-thirds had occupied their present home for less than six years, as against only one-third of the central Lagos householders. They were, therefore, much less close to their kin; about three-quarters of their surviving parents lived outside Lagos, and half of the householders with brothers or sisters had none living in Lagos. Their relatives in the town mostly formed part of their household—a young brother or sister, for instance, come for schooling, and to help about the house—and they had few close relatives elsewhere on the mainland, fewer still on the Island. There is probably no part of the town, outside the old district of Lagos Island, with its characteristic intimacy and social cohesion.

Such, then, is the distinctive setting of family life in central Lagos. Here and there, a family group still shares in common a home left to them by the founder of their lineage in Lagos. But for the most part, the household had displaced the compound as the predominant unit of residence. Two-thirds of the residents are tenants, who, though long established, still have family ties with their birthplace. But the households are not isolated: their connections branch out into the neighbourhood, and their lives are still centred on the affairs of their family group.

3

THE CONDUCT OF FAMILY AFFAIRS

VISITING

SINCE most of the residents of central Lagos have widespread family connections in the neighbourhood, the family can be held together by a day to day exchange of visits. News is passed on, problems discussed as they arise, and the comfort of old people is ensured by the small presents in cash or kind brought for them by their kinsfolk. Many people walk to work, calling on relatives along the way. 'I see my mother every day,' said a clerk in one of the big commercial firms, 'I knock on her door every morning on my way to work, and tell her, "Good morning, Mother," and again in the afternoon.' In the early evening, after a rest and a change of clothes, he might stroll out for further calls—'you have your supper, and you think, I'd like to go and see my sister. And you come back in an hour's time and tell your wife, I've been to see my sister, see my aunt, see my brothers . . .' Sometimes he went with his wife to call on her family—six brothers and three sisters, all nearby—if she had not been there earlier in the day. 'She goes to see them morning, afternoon and evening—in the morning to see them, and if she misses them in the afternoon, we go together in the evening, arm in arm.' Often several members of the family foregather casually as they make their nightly round of visits. 'That's how it is amongst our people,' said a labourer, who came from a village near Ilorin, 'we visit each other, and sit at leisure and talk over everything we have on our minds. If there's a dispute, we can settle it for those concerned. And if a bottle of beer should happen to find its way amongst us, we dispose of that too.'ᵞ[1] His widowed father was at his home town, but he had

[1] The symbol ᵞ indicates that the passage quoted has been translated from Yoruba.

28

four half-brothers, two half-sisters, and several uncles living nearby, apart from a younger brother who had a room in the same house. Both his wives, too, though they were born in the same town as himself, had many brothers and sisters in the neighbourhood. He visited them less regularly than his wives, but they often met casually in the street. It is nothing uncommon, in central Lagos, to meet twenty of your kinsfolk in the course of an ordinary day.

Apart from those born in Lagos, most of the men and women interviewed also maintained close ties with their home town, and returned there as often as time and money allowed. Many people with family connections at Ibadan or Abeokuta spend a week-end there once or twice a month, or some of their relatives from up-country visit them for the day. 'On Sunday the family will come,' said a prosperous shoemaker, 'you know we Yoruba are not like white people, we do not wait to be invited. If I have a brother in Abeokuta, his son may come, let us say, or a cousin. So in the afternoon there is fried yam, beer for an aged person, Coca Cola for the children. It is because of our belief that in this way they will help us when we are old, and when you die, they will remember their uncle who did this or that for them. That is why we are careful never to offend them, and treat them like that so they will never forget it.' Salaried workers would spend their fortnight's annual leave at home or, if it was far, save their entitlement for a longer visit every other year: traders and inde-pendent craftsmen could travel more freely, but they too tended to make their visits long rather than frequent, because of the expense.

The cost is not only in fares, but the gifts that will be expected. A woman trader who was born in Awe—about 150 miles from Lagos—explained, 'I can't go to my town more than once a year. It's a great expense for people living in Lagos to make frequent visits home. There, they think anyone from Lagos has a mint of money, and however niggardly you are they'll get money or clothes from you. Early in the morning, you'll see old women filling your water pots—it wouldn't do for a visitor to arrive home one day and have to go about fetching water the next. And when you've given them something, there will be others asking what you've brought from Lagos. Some ask for bread, others for money, or clothes like a blouse or headtie which you've hardly worn. It's a great expense, and you can't get out of it. If you refuse you get a bad name amongst your people. We've nowhere to hide.'[Y] Some of the young men, particularly, try very hard to live up to their assumed prosperity, and mortgage several months' salary to equip themselves with smart new clothes before they make a visit home. Because of these expenses, the maintenance of close ties between members of a family depend a good deal on their nearness to each other.

When people return to their home town, they speak of visiting their family, rather than any particular relative. They will call on all their kin, with presents for each. The exchange of visits, whether daily or annual, fulfils a social obligation to the group as a whole: it expresses a common loyalty as much as the personal affection of the members for each other.

But some relationships are naturally the closest, especially between children and their mother. As one young man observed, 'not only ourselves, everywhere in Nigeria, and I could say in the whole world, it is like that—we have more affection for the mother. It is because when we are small our mothers care for us more than our fathers.' In the larger sample, almost half the mothers of those interviewed were seen daily, but only 28% of the fathers—and though fewer of the fathers were living nearby, the difference is not as great as in the frequency with which their children saw them. Especially when the father has several wives, he is likely to be less intimate with his children. Over 70% of the householders interviewed were born to fathers with children by different wives, and several had thirty or even fifty brothers and sisters living. 'My father had twenty-one sons, not counting the girls,' remarked a man of fifty. 'You know in those days they packed wives like sardines.'

Brothers and sisters are united through their relationship with their mother, rather than their father. The nearer they lived to her, the more they saw of each other, and they met less often after she was dead. Ties between children of the same father but different mothers were less close. Nearly half the householders with full brother alive saw at least one of them daily, and 27% saw a sister: the proportion of both half brothers and half sisters seen as often is less by 10%.[1]

But the cohesion of the family does not depend upon the

---

[1] A fuller analysis of contacts between relatives is given in the statistical summary Appendix I.

strength of particular relationships, so much as the mutual affection and sense of obligation of all its members to the whole. A man may see more of his nieces than his own daughters, if he has assumed a special responsibility for them. A woman may feel a greater obligation to her aunt than her mother, if her aunt has paid for her education. Affection, dependence, responsibility are diffused over a wide range of kin.

MEETINGS AND CELEBRATIONS

The more formal occasions which bring the family together express its unity even more clearly than the regular exchange of visits. Funerals, weddings, naming ceremonies are the concern of all the kin, to which they will contribute their share. In Lagos they are becoming family parties, where the foregathering of relatives is more important than the rituals which mark the phases of life. There is a popular convention that members of the same branch of a family should appear together identically dressed (*aso ebi*). A cloth is chosen some weeks beforehand, and made up specially for the occasion. The effect is often very charming, and symbolizes strikingly the unity of the family.

Every family will try to make as much of these occasions as their resources will allow, and if they are properous, with a social position to maintain, they may spend several hundred pounds. Here is a description of the funeral party of a distinguished old man in the neighbourhood of this study. It may help to suggest the lavish hospitality and gaiety of a Yoruba funeral, which does not mourn a loss, but rather commemorates a long life well lived.

> Only an obituary notice posted by the porch, already torn and faded, brought death to mind. The party filled the whole lane from end to end. Chairs and tables were laid out in squares and lines, with here and there a table stacked with beer bottles. The neighbour's wives squatted by their stalls of cola nuts and cigarettes, almost amongst the guests. The most distinguished guests sat under a shelter of matting, with bottles of beer and whisky before them. A gramophone was blaring at full volume from the porch behind, and two or three portly middle-aged men were jigging to the music, glass in hand—the son of a chief, a business man, a retired customs official. After a while, more people stood up to dance, and two

beautifully dressed matrons joined them. They were clothed identically, in smoke-blue muslin blouses over a light blue velvet wrap, with a sash of blue and buff. Under the wrap showed the lace fringe of a peacock blue petticoat. They both wore white scarves over their purple head ties, to show that they were Hajas—women who have made the pilgrimage to Mecca. The groups sitting on the benches began to break up more informally. Further down the lane, a group of drummers was strolling among the tables. Children were looking on, collecting beer bottle tops, or fetching and carrying bottles, glasses, plates of rice and stewed meat in sauce.

The party must have cost several hundred pounds. The loudspeaker, benches, glasses were hired from a firm who specialise in these arrangements. There was beer or whisky for several hundred people. And apart from the food or drink, it is the custom for the women guests to come forward and ask for money. A shilling or two shillings is pressed into the forehead, a gesture of thanks to them for coming. The celebration had been continuous since the burial eight days before, ending in this climax. It would be followed by another forty days later. If the family could afford it, they would thereafter hold an annual commemoration. Only those senior to the deceased kept apart from the easy cheerfulness of the occasion.

The funeral of a distinguished figure from a large and prosperous family is the biggest of Lagos social occasions. But weddings too, as everywhere in the world, are celebrated in style. And the naming of a new born child is also an important occasion. According to Yoruba custom, the ritual should be performed by an elder eight days after the birth, with calabashes of gin, honey, sugar, pepper and cola nuts. The nuts are broken, and the pieces cast to read the child's future. Then the child's mouth is touched by the food from each pot. In a Christian household, the ritual will be preceded by prayers. But many people no longer follow the traditional forms, preferring to throw a party sometimes in the first weeks after the child is born.

Apart from these celebrations, many families hold regular formal meetings—sometimes weekly, or on a Sunday of the month—to discuss their affairs. Amongst the heads of households interviewed, 61% attended such meetings regularly in the course of the year—18% weekly, and 34% monthly. The proportion is highest for those born in Lagos: 69% had regular meetings at least once every month. Others who had few relatives in Lagos attended only gatherings at their home town once or twice a year.

Some were small councils of parents and children, but more commonly there would be a dozen to thirty present, occasionally over a hundred. Less frequent meetings tend to be larger: a Muslim family which foregathered at their Abeokuta home at the annual Biram festival, amounted to hundreds—'everyone will come, uncles, children, grandchildren, women. If you see the house then—Jesus!'

These meetings differ both in their organisation and their purposes. The large annual gatherings are held mostly so that kinsfolk may know and recognise each other. Apart from the pleasure of renewing family ties, this has a practical importance: Yoruba marriages are strictly exogamous, and a match between kin could occur through ignorance of the relationship. A member of an Abeokuta family, for instance, explained that a general meeting was to be held shortly because, 'my father has about forty-eight children, and we do not all know each other. We shall summon all of us to Abeokuta, so that we are all acquainted and do not marry our children to each other: and so that we can talk about our father's property.' The more frequent meetings generally raise a subscription of a few shillings, minutes are taken, and officers elected from time to time. The money raised may be used to help members of the family in need, or set aside towards the building or repair of a family house, or even the running of a corporate business in the name of the founder. 'We want to rent a shop, and sell provisions, and put up the signboard in my father's name,' said one of a family of eleven children, whose father had died ten years before.

Some of these meetings have only recently been organised on a formal basis. Now that family property has become a capital asset as well as a home, it needs more deliberate management. Some of the educated members of the family may suggest a formal constitution with elected officers, to regulate procedure in their common interests. For instance, the owner of a small export firm has initiated the organisation of both his father's and mother's family meetings, to which he acted as secretary. Both were long-established Lagos families. On his father's side they met quarterly, and the senior members were expected to contribute two pounds a month, the junior members one pound. Although there were over a hundred members, the payment was not always regular, and contributions amounted in practice to about £45 a month: a special levy could be made in emergency. The union was responsible for helping its members with marriages, funerals, naming ceremonies, and in sickness and unemployment. It would also try to find jobs. About sixty members came to these meetings, which were held at his home, including representatives from outside Lagos. Besides these quarterly meetings, they would also meet informally for a feast. His mother's side met on the last Saturday of each month, at the same place, and subscribed 10s.: forty to fifty usually attended.

In some families, only the more senior members attend the usual business meetings. A young clerk explained, 'I only go when I have the chance, because my brother of the same mother will be there to represent me, and he will have the same thoughts as I do.' At the general monthly meeting, only the senior members attended, 'those who are strong in family talks'. More comprehensive meetings were held from time to time, when all concerned would be circularized by letter.

Even the small meetings sometimes adopt a formal procedure, with minutes and agenda, to discuss their personal affairs. The four adult brothers of a family, for instance, had been meeting regularly with their mother and father once a month since 1954. The second brother, a teacher, was their secretary, and he gave the following account of their recent discussions:

At the last meeting? Mostly about the eldest. He's not getting much to do now, in the way of family responsibilities, and I thought he might be in a better position to assist. I'm supporting my brother in college, and the expenses are a heavy burden to me. But unfortunately there was no-one could assist me. The meeting before that—that was mostly about a younger brother of mine, the metal fitter. He wanted to get into a Government department or firm, and do other private jobs as well, and that way get something tangible. So we went to the Labour department to ask for him. No, we haven't found anything yet, but we are making enquiries. Before that? I don't remember—but I can think of one thing, that is the most important—a dispute between my father and my mother. My mother is a woman of many organisations, and she is often out. When my Dad comes home from work, the boys attend to him, and he complained that the attentions were not properly done. So we said that she should check up and see that all things were properly set up and ready before she left for any church meeting or organisation.

There was also a wider meeting of about twenty relatives three or four times a year, at the home of his mother's father. At this meeting they discussed 'mostly someone seeking for help—old cousins, old uncles. Someone gets up and asks to assist this one—he's old, got no helper—assist the other. The subscription is according to our pockets, or he promises. At times I give one pound, at times ten shillings. Last time I gave only five shillings.' His own father also attended, besides himself and his brothers—'the family joins together making one'. But this is certainly unusual: as a rule, husbands and wives do not take part in the affairs of each other's families. As someone remarked at this interview, 'No man would interfere in the affairs of his wife's family, it would be a sort of disgrace. Unless there was some special emergency or dispute, when they might be summoned to give their decision.' However, the teacher said, 'No, it's not unusual, or perhaps it is, but my father and mother when they were young were both of the same area, and their parents had deep friendship. So my father was often in the house of his wife's parents, and he even used to eat and sleep there at times'— an explanation which satisfied everyone present. His own wife, however, had her own family meeting, which he did not attend. 'That is mostly in Lagos. When discussions are made in Lagos, she or someone will be sent to Abeokuta (where she was born) to carry the message.'

These family meetings, then, take place on several levels— the annual gatherings of fifty or a hundred kinsfolk; the more frequent councils of a lineage or its branch; regular discussions between parents and children. Relatives by marriage are generally excluded from business meetings, and more junior members of the family are sometimes represented by their seniors. Most meetings adopt a formal procedure with minutes, and elected officers, and raise a small subscription. Their main concern is mutual help, especially for the support of old people, and the management of family property: but the larger occasional gatherings also serve to acquaint the members of the kin group with each other. Such meetings may well become increasingly common, as the family disperses into separate households living in different places. The meeting replaces some of the functions of the compound: when kin no longer live together, they look for new forms of association. In the sample of households the tenants, who had fewer relatives sharing the same house than owners, tended more often to hold family meetings every week. In several instances, too, meetings had become regularised after the death of a parent, as if to ensure that brothers and sisters would not drift apart when the head of the family was gone, at whose home they had most often met.

MUTUAL HELP

The most practical expressions of family loyalty are the regular sums given for the support of kinsfolk. Seventy per cent of the heads of households interviewed gave some regular help to at least one member of their family outside their household, apart from wives or dependent children, and 55% said that they gave an average of over a pound a month. Since most of them earned less than £20 a month, and over a third less than £11, the contribution was a substantial part of their income. About a quarter spent regularly over £4 a month on relatives, and 12% over £6. These sums did not include occasional gifts, or the expenses of family ceremonies. Most of the help went to old people—parents and grandparents, uncles and aunts and elderly cousins, the widow of a father without children of her own, elderly relations by marriage. Six of the householders gave regular help to members of their grandparents' generation, 52 to their parents' generation. Apart from old people, their main responsibility was the education of younger brothers, cousins, nephews or nieces, occasionally a married sister or a brother who was relatively less well-off. Twenty-four were helping relatives of their own generation, nine those of their children's age group. But of all relatives, by far the most generally accepted responsibility was for the mother—'anyone who doesn't help his mother is a bad son', as it was said. Three-quarters of the householders, whose mother still lived, regularly supported her: in most of the other families, the old lady was herself a wealthy woman in a position to help her children. After their mothers, people most often gave help to brothers, aunts, fathers or sisters in that order. Women support their relatives as well as men, and a wife will try to set aside something for her family from her housekeeping or trade: but except for the wealthy traders, the amounts are less.

The heaviest responsibility tends to fall on the eldest son. He may have quite a lot to do, even while his father is still working.

'I am wholly responsible for my younger brother—his clothes, feeding, pocket money, everything except school fees,' said an assistant accounts clerk. He also sent his mother £2 a month, £1 to an elder sister who had left her husband, and a gift about three times a year to 'an old woman, my mother's sister, who sends requests at times, when I send her money—about two pounds ten. Or at least, I send two pounds and some other things to augment it, so it comes to about two pounds ten'. As for his father, 'I don't send him money, only presents at times—gin, or cups and accessories like that—because he is well off. My dad would be able to help me if I needed it, but I've never had such an experience yet.' Once the father is dead, the eldest son steps into his place as head of the family, and the others will look to him first for help. 'He is acting as a father to us', a younger man said of his most senior brother. 'Whether it will cost twenty pounds or thirty pounds, he is the one who will pay. I remember when my wife was sick, the doctor charged us fifty pounds, and he is the one who paid. Even I asked him not to pay, but he said he would do it, acting as a father to us, so that we would do the same for his son. Then my senior brother gives each of my wives one pound ten a month of his own account. And if my wife has anything to buy, she will contact my senior brother, who will do it for her.' The same elder brother had spent £200 on the wedding of his sister. Both brothers were employed as skilled craftsmen, at a little over £200 a year: the younger actually made slightly more. Partly for this reason, he had insisted on relieving his elder brother of responsibility for their mother.

But if one member of the family has been outstandingly successful, he will be expected to bear the largest share irrespective of seniority. The youngest of four sons, a well-to-do shopkeeper, explained, 'On my father's side I'm the only one who, I can say, God has helped. So they depend on me. Any time they need anything they can send for me. Every week I go to Abeokuta there are some elderly people I must give to.' Another wealthy man, apart from supporting a very large household, and two children in England, helped to maintain an invalid elder brother, three nephews, a niece and two surviving wives of his father who had no children of their own. Such responsibilities, once accepted, cannot be dropped, even though the relationship is not close: as one man remarked of two young cousins of his mother to whom he gave three to four pounds monthly, 'I must be there every month. They have no one else.'

Where possible, however, the obligations will be adjusted to fall fairly on each of the earning members of the family, especially if the commitment cannot be held over in a difficult month. 'When my father was working, any one of us at the end of the month might give him something, but not to the knowledge of the others,' said one of three brothers. 'But for the past year or so he has been sick. We pay the rents and finance him. The three of us contribute ten pounds a month—it's shared equally.'

Besides these regular sums, there are many occasional calls for help—an uncle has been unable to finish a new house, and each of the family subscribes a few pounds to meet the balance; doctor's fees; a present for a visitor from your home town; funds for a relative who wants to set up in business; marriage payments. Sometimes the money is given more from a sense of loyalty than any urgent need—'my real brother at times demands money from me—five pounds or ten pounds—not frequently because he is doing work too. But as a brother I must show it to him.' And some received as much help as they gave, or depended on others to help them discharge their responsibilities. 'When I'm in need of help, and I'm not in the power to do it myself, only my elder brother, if he has it, he will help me. When I went on leave, I asked him to give me something to take to the family. It was roughly ten pounds as we have a large family. I requested it from him and he gave it to me just as dash—[a present]—for myself to give them.' Some therefore, who gave quite large sums, were themselves supported: while others, who might give less, were struggling alone to maintain a very heavy burden of responsibilities. In prosperous families, where the old people have a substantial income from rents, the reciprocal exchange of gifts tends to balance up, and entails no hardship. In a poor family, a senior member with a regular income may have to deny himself even the smallest luxuries for the sake of his kin.

These obligations are not undertaken disinterestedly: in giving help, people recall what their parents, aunts and uncles did for them, and hope that their children's generation will support them in their turn. 'I worked very hard when I was young,' said an elderly widow. 'Now my daughter here cooks for me. A person who has worked must rest. My children pay for my food and light and washing. I've done as much for them: I brought them up since they were small, and married the senior ones to good wives. They can't leave me to suffer now.'ᵞ Among the heads of households interviewed, fourteen were receiving regular sums worth, on average, about four pounds a month. Six were elderly widows, and one a retired arabic teacher of seventy-four, supported by their children. A middle aged man, convalescing from a long illness, was maintained by his brothers, who also paid for consultations with two private doctors. The remainder were mostly younger women, living apart from their husbands, and one or two young men, just starting in business, whose older relatives supplemented their earnings.

The family group, therefore, assumes responsibility for the welfare of its members: as yet, there are few public services in Nigeria to relieve it of any of these duties. A strong sense of mutual obligations sustains ties of kinship as the dominant concern of everyday life. Every member of the family group has a status, rights and obligations, and enjoys the sense of security which comes from these. He is protected against unemployment, old age, the cost of sickness, and can appeal to it in any difficulty. In return, he will be expected to support others, to contribute to family celebrations, to attend meetings, and reciprocate visits.

TRIBAL AND FRIENDLY SOCIETIES

This loyalty to ties of kinship also protects the newcomer to Lagos, since, though he may have no close relatives in town, he can claim upon remoter connections. Moreover, immigrants from distant towns sometimes compensate for lack of relatives by quasi-family ties with people from their home town or village, who have established themselves in Lagos. Tenants tend in time to gather their own countrymen around them, and they may refer to each other as 'brothers', even though no direct relationship can be traced between them. For the mutual welfare of the family group, and regular family meetings, they substitute associations of people born in the same village or district, which afford similar protection.

The Ibo from the Eastern Region, especially, have a very well organised system of meetings. Coming from an overcrowded country, they have travelled most widely all over Nigeria, and established associations in every major city, based

on their own political traditions. Unlike the Yoruba, they are
not town dwellers. The basic social unit is a hamlet of scattered
homesteads, which may comprise only brothers and their wives
and children, or larger groups related patrilineally. Several such
hamlets form a 'village'. These villages are in turn grouped
around a common meeting place, and were traditionally, for
most purposes, the highest political unit. But they are sometimes
organised into larger groups which share a common name and
consider themselves as being of the same loosely conceived
clan.[1] Ibo in Lagos belong to meetings which correspond roughly
with these three groupings—village, village group, and clan.
Those with enough representatives of their own home neighbourhood will hold a 'family' meeting, though the members may not
be directly related, and the members of this meeting will come
from the same cluster of hamlets, which form a 'village'. One of
the Ibo householders interviewed, for instance, belonged to a
'family' meeting which met monthly, and raised subscriptions of
sixpence a time. Attendance was about thirty, and the funds were
used for mutual help in sickness, unemployment or bereavement.
He also belonged to a monthly 'town' meeting—'town' corres-
ponds with the village group: towns in the Eastern Region are
in many cases market and administrative centres rather than
concentrations of people, who lived dispersed in their homesteads
throughout the area. Any member of the 'family' meeting could
also attend the town meeting, where the subscription was 1/6*d.*,
and attendance over a hundred. Much of the money collected
here was sent home to provide scholarships, roads, schools and
hospitals—some of these associations describe themselves as
Improvement Leagues or Progressive Unions.[2] 'But we don't

---

[1] See Daryll Forde and G. I. Jones, *The Ibo and Ibibio speaking peoples of South-Eastern
Nigeria.*

[2] For example a list of societies meeting regularly at one community centre comprised:

Okrika Progressive Union	Ikwerre National Congress
Edo Youth League	Okpala Area Meeting
Umuaka Family Meeting	Mbwasi Group Union
Abagana Welfare Union	Onitsha Youth League
Eleke Improvement Union	Benin National Union
Asaba Union	Uromi People's Congress
Udi Divisional Union	Abonema Youth League
Ora Youth Association	Ishan Progessive Union
Ngwa Clan Union	Ibusa Union
Central Ngwa Union	Okpe Youth Club

send all the money home, we keep the rest in case of any accidents to one of our members—well, you know, either death or trouble. If he comes purposely to borrow money, he will refund it, but if the trouble is beyond his pocket or his savings, we give it and tell him not to pay. In the case of death we carry out all the responsibilities, sending his property home, buying ground for burial, and if he has a wife then we send the wife home.' Part of the funds were also allocated to a divisional association, which covered a wider area, and to which each of the affiliated local unions sent representatives.

These meetings are not confined to Ibo. Other easterners have similar organisations, and some of the Yoruba towns have associations of their people in Lagos—which do not, however, generally send much money home. The northerners do not attach so much importance to these associations for mutual welfare. The Nupe meet weekly in central Lagos, but no regular subscription is raised, and attendance seems to be casual. Unlike the Ibo, there was no fear of ostracism if they ignored the organisations of their fellow countrymen in the town.

Besides these meetings, there are many friendly societies in Lagos which, in return for a regular subscription, give help to members—expecially to meet the cost of family ceremonies. Many of these groups are small, a few friends who have grown up together and meet regularly socially as well as for mutual welfare. Others are modelled on masonic lodges, or trade associations. A third of the householders interviewed in central Lagos belonged to such an organisation. A skilled craftsman, for instance, belonged to a group of a dozen, all friends from youth and neighbours, who met every Sunday morning. Two were traders, the rest wage earners. They subscribed a shilling a week, and paid two guineas to any member celebrating a naming ceremony in his family, one guinea for a marriage, and 10s. 6d. for a funeral. The members of the group would also attend the ceremony, paying their own expenses. The order of payments is unusual: in most societies the grant for funerals is the highest, typically two guineas. The society also made loans on occasions to members who were unemployed, and paid a share of doctors' fees if they were sick. A member of a butchers' society, where the subscription was half a crown a week, received five guineas from them when he was sick.

Many of these societies meet for entertainment as well as mutual welfare: some meet by rotation at each other's houses, when the host must provide hospitality out of his own pocket. If the members are expected to have some standing, the social obligations may be heavy, and membership of such societies is sometimes chiefly a means to further a career. A sanitary inspector belonged to a court of the Reformed Ogboni society: traditionally, the Ogboni were a powerful and semi-secret political organisation of the Yoruba city states, but the Reformed society is now, as he described it, 'a kind of freemasons'. The subscription was ten shillings a month, and the qualifications for membership included integrity, punctuality and a degree of seniority. The society would help to find work for members, particularly in Government service, and assist them in difficulties.

But even if he does not join any association, no newcomer to Lagos is likely to be altogether isolated. He will find someone on whose hospitality he can make a claim, as kinsman or country-man. As he becomes established, through friends, his mosque, his church, by inviting relatives to join him, he will become integrated into social life. Nor will he lose by this his sense of belonging to a particular family, region or people. The organisa-tion of Lagos society emphasises rather than replaces these original loyalties. Through them, he finds his place in the structure of small groups by which relationships are defined and given purpose.

However, only those with a wide circle of kin in Lagos belong wholeheartedly to the society in which they live and work, since family ties are the most compelling loyalty in personal affairs. Despite the gradual decay of the family compound as a common residence of the lineage, the group of kin have maintained their cohesion through their nearness to each other, their day to day contacts, the meetings and celebrations by which they assert their corporate identity. The group has essential practical functions: to organise and promote the welfare of its members, to care for its dependants, to supervise its common interests. But also, through their sense of belonging to the family as a whole, people find an emotional security which a European would look for rather in particular relationships. The way in which this affects the obligations and expectations of marriage is considered in the next chapter.

4

MARRIAGE

IN NIGERIA, marriages may be contracted by customary law, in church, or by civil ceremony. A customary marriage is solemnized by the consent of the bride's family, and was traditionally arranged between the kinsfolk of the couple: the bridegroom usually presents the family of the bride with an agreed sum, and ritual gifts.[1] Church and civil marriages entail rights and penalties derived from English rather than Nigerian custom: polygamy becomes a crime, and the wife has personal rights in divorce and as a widow foreign to African traditions. Church weddings also tend to be more expensive, and become commoner with education and social standing. In Lagos, most Christians as well as Muslims contract marriages under customary law, and even those who are wed in church may observe many of the traditional customs. Nearly all the householders interviewed in central Lagos were, or had been married, and a third of them were Christian. But only a quarter of the Christians had married in church.

GETTING MARRIED

In all, the householders had contracted 126 current marriages,

[1] Traditionally amongst the Yoruba, 'Betrothal takes place at an early age, after consultation of the *Ifa* oracle. For a first marriage the parents of the boy send the first instalment of the marriage payment to make the formal betrothal (*ijohun*). The boy makes periodic gifts of yams and maize to the girl's father and helps with manual work. Gifts of goods and services are also made on special occasions. The final marriage payment is called *idana*. After *idana* has been paid the date of the marriage is arranged, the carrying of the bride to her husband's house being known as *igbeyawo*. She is accompanied by her age mates and two wives of her extended family, who remain with her until the wedding night. She is lifted on the shoulders of a former bride of her extended family, and carried into her husband's compound. This is still the custom amongst the Oyo and Egba.'
Daryll Forde, *The Yoruba-speaking Peoples of South-Western Nigeria*, p. 28.

and of these only seven had been Christian marriages, and one a civil ceremony. Two-thirds of the marriages were between men and women of the same birthplace, and one man alone had married a woman of different ethnic origin. He maintained, 'It doesn't matter whom you marry, you can marry someone from anywhere. It's just a matter of the character and qualities of the woman.' But in practice a wife from a strange tribe is not likely to be at home with her husband's family, and differences of custom may make difficulties. In one or two instances, a man who was unable to return to his home town to look for a wife had commissioned a relative or a trustworthy older woman to find a wife there for him, rather than pick a Lagos girl. Marriages between men and women of different places were commonest when one or other had been born in Lagos.

Four-fifths of the men had chosen their wives themselves: even in first marriages, only a quarter had left the initiative to their parents, though they would commonly ask their help in arranging the match. 'I went home and saw the lady, and then I told my parents, and they went there to see if it was a good family, and after they had found out, I went home and married her.' This is now a more usual order than the experience of a young Yoruba from Ilorin district, who explained, 'According to our tradition parents have to give out their children for marriage from youth. The parents will be in touch, even though the children do not know each other. When I came to Lagos, I was told by my parents to look out for them (his wife's parents) because I was to marry into their family. That way, the members of the family will know each other on both sides from the first, so the marriage will prosper.' A Yoruba craftsman from Porto Novo had married his daughter to a man of his birthplace. 'I gave her away, she didn't choose her own husband. I wanted my name to be remembered over there.' But he agreed, 'It's certainly difficult nowadays to find a daughter that would do that. They all want to marry the men they've taken a fancy to, instead of their parent's choice. That's why I'm particularly fond of her.'[Y]

Traditionally, marriages were sometimes arranged when the girl was still a child—or even, occasionally, provisionally contracted with a child still unborn—especially in the East and North. A young Ibo of twenty-three corresponded regularly with a girl of fifteen at his birthplace, whom he had met on his last visit home four years before. He expected to marry her in a few years' time, though they were not formally engaged: 'It's serious in the sense that I don't think of disappointing her, and she doesn't think of disappointing me'. Only one of the householders interviewed had actually married a girl before puberty: he was a Hausa trader, born in Lagos, twenty-five years old. At the age of seventeen he had married a girl of nine, and their first child was born when she was fourteen. He admitted, 'The public were against it. They said—the public and the people at the maternity hospital—why should you have a child like that going about with a man?'

The marriage payments varied from place to place, and according to circumstances. A management trainee who married into a distinguished Abeokuta family offered £60, but his father-in-law, after complimenting him on the amount, told him to keep the money and instead gave his daughter an equivalent sum. An Itsekiri man from Warri explained, 'We are not so particular about money there. If the fathers loves you, he will give you his daughter, and you may just take him some present. In the old days it was a few bottles of gin and cola nuts. And the rest is between yourself and your wife.' A native doctor paid only five and seven pounds to the parents of two of his wives because, 'I helped to cure these two women when they were sick, and when they regained their health, their parents agreed that I should marry them, and I gave them only a small sum for the purpose.'[1] At the other extreme were payments of over a hundred pounds. The average was £28: the largest sums were paid in Abeokuta, where the average was £35. In Lagos it was about £20, and elsewhere in Yoruba country a pound or so less.[1] The payments on the marriage of a first wife were on average about five pounds more than later marriages.

The expenses of the wedding itself—in gifts and entertainments—are likely to be considerably more than the marriage payment. Indeed, extravagant weddings have become a social problem. I once watched a street play, acted by members of the Federal Social Welfare Department, dramatizing the folly of ostentation. In the first scene, the hero complains that he wants

[1] The numbers are too small to suggest the averages for other parts of Nigeria, but the sums paid were mostly less than this, and amongst the Hausa sometimes only a few pounds.

45

to marry, but where is he to find the money? Take the girl and never mind the marriage, says his worldly adviser. But if she has a child? Send her back to her parents and claim the child later. But the hero himself has suffered from being separated from his mother and brought up by a stepmother, and rejects this advice. In the second scene, the girl agrees to have him, but insists on a lavish wedding in family dress, and will hear nothing of his protests that he cannot afford it. So he borrows £200 from a money lender and marries in style, and of course is ruined when he cannot pay. Remorsefully, his spoilt young wife recognizes her folly, and a commentator points the moral. The audience appreciated the play: some blamed lax parents, some the men for boasting that they were richer than they were, some the grasping Lagos girls, some the fashion for competitive consumption. At one performance, no woman would at first come forward to give an opinion: finally, a practical young woman suggested that the foolish husband should have saved his £200, and spent £5 on a love potion instead.

A member of a well-to-do Lagos family told me he would try to marry in England, as soon as he'd qualified, to save money, 'Yes, there—it's much cheaper. If you get married here it's too expensive. First of all you send a letter to the bride's parents and then you have a thanksgiving when your letter is accepted, and buy food and drinks. And then there's the bride price: if you've been to England, it might be £50. Then a few days before the wedding there's the engagement party. Then there's the reception after the wedding, and in the evening there's a party at the bride's house and the bridegroom's house. Champagne—yes, we have champagne too, and sometimes you have to buy clothes for the women. I don't know how much it would all cost—I think some hundreds of pounds.' There is also a custom that women of the bride's family spread their head ties before the bridegroom as he leaves the church or mosque, and invited him to step on them. Before he does so, he is expected to throw money on the ground for them, which may be several pounds before they are satisfied. He may be unlucky enough to meet a second group waiting for him at the doors of the reception hall. 'I began to feel this was too much,' as one bridegroom complained. 'I said to them, "if I am to give you so much, your sister will have to suffer when we get to Lagos," and everyone laughed.

Even my wife told me not to listen to them, it was getting too much.' The custom symbolises, perhaps, the reluctance of the wife's kin to part with her, for which they demand compensation.

The expenses of the bridegroom at the wedding averaged double his marriage payment, which suggests that display is now more important than the gifts which seal the contract. To set a high price on the marriage payment becomes merely a means of asserting wealth or status, and as such may be despised by a family which is sure of its social standing, and would prefer to see the money spent on setting their daughter up in her new home. Since, too, most men and women now choose each other independently of their families, the making of the payment no longer binds the two groups of kin so much together. Traditionally, the marriage payment was a surety, as well as a compensation to the woman's family for the loss of their daughter. It protected the wife, since if her husband turned her out without reason, he would not be able to reclaim his payment, which he might need to replace her. It protected the husband, since his wife's family, not wishing to return the payment, would use their influence to see that she gave no grounds for divorce. But few Lagos husbands now attempt to reclaim the marriage payment if they separate from their wives. 'We in Lagos, we don't usually demand anything,' said a man who had been deserted twice. 'If you've enjoyed yourselves together for a period of years, what is the necessity of demanding money?' He had paid seven guineas at his first marriage, by which he had no children, and five at the second. Besides, if the marriage payment is only a minor part of the expenses, the refunding of it will not go far towards the cost of a new marriage.

POLYGAMY

Two-thirds of the householders in central Lagos were Muslim, and half the Muslim men had taken more than one wife. In a Muslim family, to have only one wife reflects a little on a man's social standing: presumably, he cannot afford more. 'Your wife's junior brother has two wives, and you have only one. How is that?' someone challenged a Muslim trader in the course of an interview. 'Ask yourself,' he replied, 'and the answer is only financial trouble.' His prestige was clearly compromised by his having only one wife when someone junior to himself had two. A fifth of the married men who described themselves as Christians also had more than one wife. Since it is widely believed that women outnumber men, some Christians think the church wrong to forbid polygamy, and do not regard it as incompatible with their faith. 'If they want to be in touch with what is going on in the world, I think they are a bit wrong,' said a Catholic, 'because God knows there are more women than men. And what will happen to the other women if each man has only one wife? It will lead to sin.' In all, 38% of the married men in the sample of householders had more than one wife.[1] Religion apart, the proportion tended to increase with income—30% of the men earning £10 or less, 49% of those earning £11 to £30, and 65% of those earning over £30 a month.

Besides prestige, there are practical and moral advantages in having several wives. The Yoruba consider it wrong to have sexual relations with a woman once she is pregnant, until the child is weaned at the age of two. It is still widely believed that semen would harm the child in the womb, and later spoil the mother's milk. The alternative to nearly three years of sexual abstinence is therefore casual relations, which many consider wrong, or a second wife. Since, too, it is common to send a pregnant woman to her mother-in-law to be looked after, and bear her child there, the husband may be left without a housekeeper for months or even years. Again, if the wife is a trader, she may often be away on business. A Catholic explained that he took a second wife because, 'My first wife is a trader, and she was often away at Port Harcourt or Sapele, or visiting her family, or she might be sick. So I was alone in the house, and I'm a man, I can't cook. Who was to look after me?' His first wife, who was also a practising Catholic, raised no objection. 'Her own father had four wives, she knows it is the custom. I gave her some cash—ten pounds—to compensate her, because the love is divided.'

Traditionally, however, the most important reason for marrying several wives was children, and parents may bring pressure to bear on their sons for the sake of the future of the family. A Muslim clerk in a commercial firm, from a long established Lagos family, observed, 'Fathers and mothers force their

[1] 48% of the larger central Lagos sample, where in all 81% were Muslim.

48

children to marry many wives because they want many grand-children. It's children they want to see. They say, "don't be selfish". But the wives don't like it. If a husband stays out late, his wife starts accusing him of looking for another wife. They don't want it. Only by force—it's war!' But he had married two wives himself, of his own choice. 'It's expensive, but I can't help it. Our fathers used to have ten wives, we can only afford two—sometimes not even two, only a half.'

It is probably true that most women in Lagos would prefer to be the only wife. But a few defended polygamy to me. 'It's good for a man to have two wives. If one is sick, the other will look after her. But if she's her husband's only wife who will look after her, who will be cooking for her husband?' An old Muslim lady said firmly, 'The only wife of a husband is a bad woman: she doesn't like her husband, otherwise she'd want company for him.'ᵞ She herself had been her husband's most senior wife: he took his second after she became pregnant for the second time. He always consulted her before he took another wife, and she would investigate the girl's family and character. She used to take presents to the girl's family—claiming the cost afterwards from her husband if she was short of money. 'That's why they all like me.' She treated them like daughters, helped them in their confinements, and showed them how to nurse their children.

In such a household, the senior wife enjoys a privileged position. She has authority over the juniors, and leaves to them the heavy housework. An old song runs, 'We shall be the senior wife. I will not be the junior who is to warm the soup, I will be the senior wife.' So long as her own position is secure, a first wife need not lose by having a helper—especially if she has had the opportunity to approve the girl beforehand. Her consent will be influenced by the tact with which her husband introduces his new wife. 'I persuaded her before,' said one husband of his senior wife. 'And I always gave her more than the second. I gave her two guineas just before the second came, and said, "this is just for you to do what you like with, and just because I have a second wife, don't think it will make any difference to what I have planned for you." ' The junior wives, of course, have no such compensations for sharing a husband, but then they accept their position, in agreeing to the marriage.

49

E

Marriage

If the wives agree together, and their husband treats them with scrupulous fairness, the household will live contentedly together. But it is more vulnerable to any change in the husband's circumstances. Wages are low, employment uncertain, traders are at the mercy of fluctuations in the market. Illness, for lack of adequate medical services, may be serious and protracted. A wife cannot be confident that her husband will always be able to support her, or that his family will be able and willing to maintain her should he fail. The risks are all the greater when the husband has several wives: not only must his resources go further, but quarrels are more likely to arise from jealousy and favouritism. The first wife may resent the newcomer as a threat to her own security, especially if she has not been consulted. Some men, besides, impose a new wife unwillingly on the more senior, fail to consult her, or even use the new marriage as a manoeuvre to drive her away. Lagos, too, like every capital city, is more conscious of fashion, and lays out in its shops and markets a greater variety of consumer goods than any other town in Nigeria. However prosperous her husband, few wives will really welcome money that might have been spent on her and her children going to another woman. As one of my informants wrote to his mother, who wanted him to take a second wife, 'Packing wives together is a pleasure at home, but in a civilized place like Lagos it is much trouble. So please do not put me to such work.' The fear that she may be ousted by a rival tends to make a wife feel less secure, more aggressive in defence of her interests, and this in itself puts more strain on the marriage.

LIVING APART

So much has been said about the instability of marriage in modern Africa, and the breakdown of traditional sanctions, it is worth emphasising that four-fifths of the marriages contracted by the householders interviewed had been successful, and the relationship between husband and wife was commonly affectionate and co-operative. But divorce is still relatively frequent— a fifth of the householders had contracted one or more marriages which failed, a higher rate than any European country. The most common causes seem to have been a wife's jealousy, her adultery, or the financial failure of the husband. A prosperous craftsman who had been married three times remarked, 'I was living with two, then after some years one went away. After I marry for the third time, after some years again the second went away. You know, you can't always tell what is in a woman's heart, just all these petty grievances. The only thing I can say is jealousy. What causes most of these separations amongst our people is either adultery or jealousy.' The wife of a clerk swindled him in a trading partnership, and left him when he lost a well-paid job. Another man admitted that he deserted both his wives when he could no longer afford to look after them: 'I stealthily left the house we were living in, until each of them looked to feed herself.'

Even when there is no question of divorce, husbands and wives may not live together, expecially if the husband has several wives. Eleven per cent of the married men were not living with any of their wives, and half the men with several wives lived apart from at least one of them. In all, a quarter of the wives were not living in their husband's household. A third of these were still in Lagos—from lack of space, or because he could not afford to maintain her, the husband had sent his wife to live with his parents or her own family, or rented her a room of her own. Two-thirds lived outside Lagos altogether.[1]

Some men had married a wife at their home town, and never brought her to Lagos. More often they sent her back there when she was pregnant, so that the child could be born under the care of its paternal grandmother. An Ijebu man explained, 'It is something traditional in our country for a pregnant woman to live with the husband's mother or relative until her delivery.' She may stay a year or two, until the child is weaned, or even longer. A wife's obligations to her own family, too, may force long separations. One husband had been waiting over a year for his mother-in-law to die, so that his wife could return to him. 'The mother—my wife is the only daughter—she's very old, and there's no-one to look after her. So I have to make that sacrifice until she breathes her last.' Shorter visits to kinsfolk were common: 40% of the wives living with their husbands had been away for over a month during the year, and 13% for more than three months.

[1] Since the interviews were with the head of each household, who would normally be the husband if present, only one of the married women interviewed was with her husband: she was assumed to be the head of the household, since they lived in her father's house. Five of the seven other husbands lived outside Lagos.

Sometimes husband and wife parted amicably in middle age, when the wife was past child-bearing. An elderly woman remarked, 'I left my husband's house after I said I would not bear any more children. I sat in peace and looked after myself. If I did not go away, who would mind about the old woman?'[Y] And a man in his sixties, 'I have had many wives before—I think they were up to six or seven. But some have died, and the rest I sent away, because now that I am old I cannot keep them any longer.' A woman looks to her family or her children, rather than her husband, to support her in her old age. If she lives in her husband's family home, she may remain there, especially if her sons are established there too: but otherwise, she may prefer to depend on her own resources. Traditionally, widows were inherited by a younger brother or other junior member of the late husband's family, but in Lagos the custom is dying out. So her ties with her husband's family tend to weaken in old age.

INDEPENDENCE AND SECURITY

In Lagos, a wife usually does not live with her husband in his family home, surrounded by his relatives, and under the authority of its head. The disappearance of the traditional compound, and the dispersal of the family into separate households, means that marriage no longer brings a wife into so close a relationship with her husband's kin. The ways in which the family group reasserts its unity—by family meetings, by visits and mutual help—bind the individual by ties of blood rather than by ties of marriage. Since, too, marriages are now less often arranged by the families of the couple, and the return of the marriage payment is often not even sought when marriages break up, the family is not so directly concerned with their success. A wife may prefer to sacrifice the support of her husband's family, for the sake of greater freedom from a system of authority where for many years she must accept a junior status. But she is less protected if some misfortune should overtake her husband, and the weakening of traditional sanctions has probably made divorce more frequent than it used to be.

A wife cannot therefore afford to become wholly dependent on her husband. She needs to secure an independent income, and this protection is very important to her. For though her own family may be able to help her, she also needs money to meet her obligations to them. Most women turn to trade, and unless their parents have already provided for them, they expect their husbands to give them capital to set up a stock. The money cannot, in practice, be returned if the marriage fails, and some men prefer to wait until they are sure of their wife, or she has borne her first child for them, before allowing her to work. A newly married man said: 'I did not allow her to trade or do any kind of work. I want her to be used to me first, and I would like to try her character before I could give her any trading capital.'ᵞ But the capital is often virtually a wedding gift from bridegroom to bride, and one of the conditions, explicitly or implicitly, of her consent.

Nine out of ten of the wives of the householders interviewed in central Lagos were working, and apart from a telephone operator and a few dressmakers, the rest were all engaged in some kind of trade—in cloth, vegetables, cooked food, tinned provisions, cigarettes. Seventy nine of them had received their initial capital entirely from their husbands, two from his family, and six had added gifts from other relatives to what their husbands gave them. Only ten had their capital from their own families, and one woman had provided for herself out of her savings. The amount varied, of course, with the husband's resources: it might be only a few pounds to buy some tinned goods or cigarettes, or a hundred pounds for a wholesale stock of bales of cloth. But the average value of this initial capital amounted to £30.

A wife's profit from her trade is her own, and she spends it mostly on her personal needs, her children, and in helping her own relatives. Households rarely pool their resources. Husbands and wives seldom know accurately, and do not expect to know, what each other earns, and the wife is not obliged to contribute to the housekeeping out of her income, even though she may earn more than her husband. But in practice she may help her husband when he is in difficulties: he gives her the initial capital partly so that he can fall back on her earnings in need. 'It is our African custom to get help from our wives when we are in difficulties, so long as we give them some money to trade with,' as one man remarked. Sometimes the money is treated as a loan, especially if it went to meet his personal expenses, or a business debt. 'At times when I lay down, they carry me up,' said a mechanic of his two wives, one a trader in cloth and the other a telephone operator, 'The reason I can manage is because I gave them capital to trade. When they see the money is not sufficient for chop, they help me out until the end of the month. Or when my money is not enough for me, they might help me and I pay them back.' A trader said: 'When we first married she wasn't working, but three years ago my mother advised me I ought to buy her a (sewing) machine. The day I gave her the machine, I also gave her twenty pounds to buy cloth, so that any time I was in difficulties she could help me. And she has helped me greatly. I reckon I am six pounds ten in her debt.' A dock labourer depended so much on his wife that he felt he could not expect her to do the housework as well. 'I can't ask her to prepare my food, since she is helping me with money. When we are both busy, I don't mind if I scarcely see her for days on end, since we depend on her earnings. She is my mother and father now.'ᵛ However, whether or not they had given them any capital, only a third of the husbands acknowledged that they received any help from their wives.

Since a woman's trade is so important to her, this, rather than her housework, gets her best attention, and she may be at her market stall from early morning until late in the evening. Some wives, too, make regular business trips to towns and villages near Lagos, which keep them away for half the month. So, although they are now more independent of their kinsfolk, husband and wives do not always spend more time together, nor has the marriage become a partnership to which both parties wholeheartedly commit their futures. Through her earnings, a wife secures an economic independence which protects her against the failure of her husband to support her.

At the same time, the younger and better educated couples are attracted towards a more companionate ideal of marriage. In the households interviewed, many young husbands not only provided their wives with a means of livelihood, but gave or lent them additional capital, bought them clothes, added pocket money to their incomes. They helped with the housework, cleaning or washing, cooking or looking after the children when their wives were busy. A clerk wrote in his diary for a Friday evening, 'About four hours spent in Mr. Okhima's bakery, where

I helped my wife by sitting with the baby, while she was busy in wrapping bread for next day's supply.' The wives, in return, helped to meet the housekeeping bills, lent money to their husband, or even maintained him altogether when his business was going badly. In marriages like this, husbands and wives are partners, rather than parties to a contract where each limits their responsibility for the affairs of the household.

It seems then that as traditional sanctions and the authority of the family group lose some of their influence, a woman may look for new safeguards in marriage of radically different kinds. On the one hand, she may try to secure greater personal independence of her husband through trade, or, if she is educated, a career. On the other hand, she may seek a relationship with her husband in which both are bound by ideals of loyalty and affection to support each other come what may. Even if her husband shares these ideals, he will not be able to provide for her with any certainty if his livelihood is insecure, and for many women their trade, or the support of her family group, can afford a better protection. But the success of a companionate marriage probably depends most on the ability of men and women to commit their feelings deeply in attachment to one person. Patterns of feeling are learned in childhood, and if children are brought up to be self-reliant, and to look for affection and support to many people rather than to one, they may still as adults expect to find emotional security above all in membership of their family group. Their childhood experiences predetermine the way in which husbands and wives adapt their relationship to new circumstances: and this in turn will influence the emphasis they place on wider family loyalties.

5

CHILDREN

WHEN Yoruba domestic life was organised around the family compound, children were brought up among the members of their lineage, under the care of uncles, aunts and grandparents, and their mother's senior co-wives, as well as their own parents. But though each household now tends to live separately, kinsfolk still care for each other's sons and daughters. If the parents cannot afford to maintain all their children, a brother, sister or cousin may take charge of them: even when the parents are not in need, they may do so as a gesture of goodwill. Old people also like to have some of their grandchildren with them, for companionship and to help with the housework, a wish which the parents could not ignore without giving offence. So children are likely now to spend more of their childhood away from home. Sometimes, too, a boy or a girl may be sent to live with a respected teacher to whom he is not related at all, paying for his training by making himself useful about the house. Since, moreover, so many wives do not live with their husbands, and perhaps a fifth of marriages fail, children often cannot share a house with both their parents. So they learn early to adjust themselves to different households, to be responsible, and to look for care and affection to others as well as their own father and mother.

Scarcely more than half the young children of the householders interviewed in central Lagos were living with both their parents, and a fifth were with neither their mother nor their father. The proportions are very similar for the children actually living in the households studied (Table III).

Children who live with only one of their parents may still, of course, see the other very often. For instance, if the father has several wives, and has rented separate accommodation for one of them, he may still be able to call every day, or his wife and

56

Children

TABLE III

WHOM CHILDREN LIVE WITH

% of children under 16 years of age living with:	children of household heads	children in household
both parents	55%	53%
mother not father	18%	15%
father not mother	7%	6%
grandparents not parents	12%	9%
other relatives only	7%	12%
non-relatives	1%	5%
Total %	100%	100%
Total number	230	246

In the households, most of the children who had no relative living with them were servants.

children will come to him. Even when the parents have separated, they will still allow each other access to their children unless the quarrel between them has been unusually bitter. Since the father always has a right to his children so long as he accepts responsibility for them, they will by custom remain under his charge. But although a woman who has left her husband hopes that he will still take an interest in their children, and further their education, it may be hard for them to live with their father and his other wives. It is generally admitted that step children are liable to suffer.[1] So, when divorced parents remarry, they may leave the children by a previous marriage in the care of

---

[1] Alison Izzett has noticed that amongst delinquent children in Lagos, the hostility of a stepmother is their commonest fear: 'Undoubtedly the greatest fear of these Yoruba delinquents is that of being harmed by the witchcraft of their father's wives, especially in cases where their own mothers are no longer living with their fathers. It is through the food given to him which has been prepared by the step-mother that the child expects harm to come and many children beg their fathers to give them money, if their mothers are not in the house to feed them, so that they may buy all their food outside the home. Many fathers agree, thus reinforcing in the child's mind his own suspicions. The jealousies of the polygamous home further strengthen the child's fears. The frequently affirmed belief that only a mother will care for her children means that any step-mother is viewed with hostility.'
Alison Izzett 'The Fears and Anxieties of Delinquent Yoruba Children', pp. 26–7.

some other relative—though a woman may prefer not to live with her new husband, so that she can keep the children with her. But divorce often means that the children of the marriage no longer live with either parent. An insurance clerk, who had three children by a woman from whom he was divorced, had sent the two younger children to his mother, who lived in Lagos nearby; and his eldest boy, aged five, to his full brother, a Post Office official stationed in the north. He was satisfied that all the children would be well looked after—'My brother picked a very good wife, she's a trained nurse, and knows all about children.'

Even when the parents have not separated, the exchange of children between relatives is an accepted custom. A well-educated clerk, who had sent his daughter to his sister, said: 'We Africans, it is our intention, if we have a female child, one may send her to the mother or sister. Though some people don't like their children to be brought up by anyone than themselves: even in my own case, it was my intention to bring up my children myself, but since I couldn't meet up all my expenses here, and she was willing, I took her to my sister.' Boys may be sent to relatives as well as girls, though it is most often the girls who go to live with a married woman of the family. In the households interviewed, where the husband was the head, two thirds of the relatives' children belonged to the wife's family—usually a girl cousin, a young sister or niece. Some of them were only a few years old when they first joined the household. Though the parents are never expected to contribute towards the maintenance of these children, beyond an occasional present, the financial relief was not necessarily the main reason for putting them out. 'I had an aunt who was on the spot when I was born,' one man said, explaining how he came to Lagos at the age of eight, 'and she loved me so much that she said I should come to live with her—and she was in Lagos.' Another man said of his wife's sister, 'The girl was young when she came here with my wife— about two or three years old then. She came so young because of the love my wife had for her.' When such children grow up, they may choose a child from the branch of the family who cared for them, and bring them up in the same way in gratitude.

In all, a quarter of the householders were caring for young children of their relatives. But the proportion is much higher amongst the women householders than the men: 52% as against 16%. Most of these were elderly widows with grandchildren.

A widow, for instance, looked after her sons' three children— a girl of twelve, and boys of ten and two. Their mother had come to live under the older woman's care, as soon as she was discharged from the maternity hospital where each child was born. She did not return to her husband's house until the children were weaned, at the age of two, by which time they were so used to their grandmother's home that she left them there. This family had been settled in Lagos for three generations, and the children's father lived no further than the next street. But immigrants also send their wives to their mother to bear her children, and the children may remain at their father's birthplace after the mother returns to Lagos. Largely for this reason, a fifth of the children born to parents from outside Lagos were not living in the city.

Some parents, apart from respecting the grandmother's wishes, thought their children would be better disciplined in the more traditional life of their home town. Older people, especially, complained that children in Lagos grew spoiled and unruly. A Yoruba Mallam in his seventies remembered the stricter discipline of his childhood, when he had been brought from Abeokuta by an aunt, to study Arabic in Lagos. 'There wasn't much playing in those days, the children were all hard-working, and competing with each other to sell for their parents. Nowadays they have more time to play, and you can't flog them now, you get arrested. In those days we used to fear the cane. For instance, there are sixty chapters in the Holy Koran,[1] and I learned to understand them all in one year, because I feared the cane. Now some children take six or seven years.' ^Y A dock worker had sent his two sons to a relative at a small town in the country, because he felt they were getting out of hand. 'Sometimes when I beat them, they'd do the same thing next day, and I was afraid that if I went on punishing them I might do them harm. That's why I sent them away. My uncle's a master bricklayer with several people under him, so he has time to keep an eye on them. They behave themselves now, they don't play truant.' ^Y

Traditional upbringing is, in principle, stern. After only a few years of indulgence and irresponsibility, children are

[1] In all, there are 114 chapters.

expected to be self-reliant and adaptable. If their home life has been unsettled, they may receive little help or understanding in their insecurity of feeling. At two they are abruptly weaned, and as soon as they are able, they are expected to make themselves useful—running errands, buying in the market, sweeping and fetching water. They may help their mother, too, with her trade. On the whole, they often enjoy their work. But the responsibility may be too great, or the load too heavy, and they may get no sympathy from a busy household if they fail. The five-year old who loses the sixpence she was to take to the market may be too frightened to go home: and there are often tears as children jostle round the public water taps, struggling to raise heavy paraffin cans of water on their heads. A young father who belonged to the N.S.P.C.C. made it his duty to help children carrying over-heavy loads, and speak to their parents, but such tasks are still generally expected of children.

Now that most Lagos children go to school, they enjoy more freedom. While their mothers are preoccupied with trade, they can enjoy themselves together on their way to and from school, and perhaps occasionally play truant. It is this freedom which parents fear, though probably most children come to little harm from it. The adventures of his childhood, described to me by a boy of eighteen, were innocent enough—even though one ended in tragedy. A few of them are quoted here for the scenes they recall of the life of a Lagos schoolboy:

> They brought out a new rule that all the truck pullers had to have a sort of brake, and they had to give their names to the police. Most of them were illiterates and couldn't write their names, so we schoolboys used to write their name and number on a piece of paper and we'd charge them sixpence each for this piece of paper with their names on. Oh, we'd make 25s. a month. It would be a funeral procession going to school, very slow and unwilling and we'd go up to all the truck-pullers we came across—and then when the police saw us we'd run.

> We had these tops, and you whipped them along the street. Each street was maybe about fifty yards. You'd whip it away, and it would fly off, and you had to try and run after it before it stopped spinning. Then you'd whip it small, small, until you came to the corner, then you'd whip it off again. You had to whip it down one street, across the road and round the corner. That was going to Mecca, and if

you could do it in three you were an Alhaji. But it was very dangerous to passers-by. You could buy the tops, or you could make them in the house, from a tread wheel, if you shaped it a bit. But they don't play with tops now. You know, in Lagos everything changes.

There was the park in the country where we used to play. One boy was killed there. He was a very good tree-climber. But he had no luck that day. In fact, we were annoyed with him. We'd send him up the tree to pick mangoes for us, but he was eating them himself. Anyway there was a branch that wasn't strong enough for his weight, and he fell and hit his head against a tomb stone. So we ran away. There was a pole and we vaulted over the wall. I was trembling when I got home in case my mother found out. The boy's mother nearly went out of her mind—he was to have been confirmed that day. It was the first time I'd ever seen anyone dead, I was seven then, and I couldn't sleep for two nights. The police went and guarded the park the next day. Then after, it might be ten weeks, one boy came on his own there with a ball and played. And the next day two or three, and the next day maybe seven of us, and then we were all back there again.

All the children love football, they stay all day on the race course there. When we played, we never admitted defeat. We used to have a shield, you know, or a cup, and when we played a match the shield would be brought to the match, and if we lost, the winners would take the shield away with them. But we never accepted defeat. If we were beaten, there was always a fight, and during the fight we'd pick up the shield and run away. Oh, we never lost our shield.

When we were late home, we used to throw a certain sort of brick against the wall which made a powder, and we believed that if we made a kind of sign on our forehead with this powder our parents would never notice anything. Well, the first two times it worked for me, but the third time I was whipped.

Another time we sold pictures of boxers, for a penny or threepence, and the very big ones a shilling. We used to cut them out of newspapers like *The Ring*. When I was server to the Bishop, I used to steal them from him—he'd have all the papers, members of the congregation would send them to him. We used to make 15*s.* a month like that.

At Christmas time there's—I don't know what you'd call it—a sort of fancy. All the boys dress up as girls, or as sailors, and go about the streets with whips. And when they meet another party like themselves they start beating them with their whips. We used to wear three pairs of long, long trousers so that we didn't feel the whips. But if you got it on the back of your head it was very painful. And people let off rockets in the cathedral when the congregation are praying, or climb up into the bell tower and ring the bell at the wrong time. And at New Year someone will come up behind you and slap you, then when you turn your head, someone slaps you in the front, and so it goes on till you have to run away. Then they wish you a happy new year.

Parents who fear that their children will be corrupted by these high spirits and petty pilfering may decide to board them out with a teacher who will supervise their education and behaviour. But there is a risk that in such a household, where the child is a servant, he may be exploited and driven to delinquency in self-protection. 'I'm thinking of an experience when I was at primary school,' one man said. 'I was brought up by my elder brother, and I lived all the time with him and he was responsible for my education and everything. Then he decided that if I stayed with him I would become uncontrollable, so I was sent to live with the headmaster. I had been happy with my brother, but now I found I had a very different kind of life. I had to get up at five o'clock every morning and sweep the whole courtyard, and cook for the man and his wife and open the wife's shop—all before I went off to school. And after a time I began to take cognizance that I was not getting enough to eat, so I took to stealing. When I sold something in the shop I would take threepence for myself. And even I knew it was wrong. But afterwards when I left that place, I gave up stealing altogether.' It seems likely that much of the delinquency of children is a reaction to the severity and lack of understanding of their guardians. Since the guardians only think of heavier punishment to suppress it, the delinquency may grow into an intense and hurtful anxiety. And parents may only make the problem worse by passing their responsibility to someone who is more interested in the child's services than his welfare.

The least protected are the children of poor parents, who leave home to become servants, not for their training, but simply to earn their keep. Ten per cent of the households studied employed servants, at a wage from 15*s*. to 30*s*. a month. Nearly all of them were girls of about twelve to fourteen, from the remoter country districts of Yorubaland, with few if any relatives in Lagos. Such housemaids are often recruited by agents, who find places for them in the cities, and ensure that they are paid a fair wage and well-treated. Sometimes they collect the girls' wages and remit them to their parents, but in the households interviewed the maids all received their own pay: in one instance, a relative had originally kept the money, 'but after a misunderstanding, I give the money into her own hand at the end of the month now, and I take her down to the bank. She keeps her own (bank) pass book.' Usually the girls collect their savings when they are about seventeen, and return home to look for a husband.

The maids in the households interviewed seemed to be cheerful and well-cared for. But far from their home and their kin, young servants cannot easily protect themselves against a harsh master or mistress except by escape. A tailor from the Eastern Region had arrived in Lagos, alone, at the age of twelve, after running away from a family who had ill-treated him. 'As a mere servant, what they give you, you must take: you have no power. If I complained, my mistress used to say, "tell your mother to bring your chop then". That used to make me angry, I told her, "I don't mind you abuse me, but not my mother". Even I left them because of hunger. The mistress sent me to market to buy many things for a journey—garri and mats, and yams. That was four-thirty in the afternoon and I had tasted nothing all day. I demanded something to eat—everyone chop twice a day, only myself never taste anything. So she began abusing me, but I wouldn't go to market. I just took what little money I had belonged to me, and went off. I came straight to Lagos, I didn't pass to my own people again.'

Both the separation of young children from their parents, and the strictness of discipline, are now beginning to be questioned. Educated parents, particularly, often prefer to bring up their own children: they worry whether, in matters of discipline, diet, or the emotional needs of their children, grandparents or other relatives will treat their children as they believe right. A senior clerk had been most reluctant to grant his mother's request to have one of his children, 'But she wanted him, and what could I do? I cannot refuse my mother.' Another clerk asked my advice, because he had been urged to send his seven-year-old son to a boarding school. 'The people here say he will get into trouble with the environment if he stays here and gets out of control.

That's what the women say.' But he had already noticed that the children seemed less happy away from home: 'Two years ago the children were with my mother-in-law, and when I moved down here I was determined to have them with me. And I noticed the change. They were happier. Before they had only very hard food, now they have tea and this one (his five-year-old daughter) can drink ten tins of milk a day. Now if you suggest they go and stay with my mother-in-law for a few days, they don't want to go.'

The Social Welfare Department, which deals with over a thousand Lagos children a year in need of care and protection, is concerned at the evidence of widespread emotional insecurity amongst children. If the argument put forward by Dr. Bowlby[1] and others is accepted, that a child may suffer lasting damage to its emotional development if separated at an early age from its mother, many Lagos boys and girls must grow up with their ability to form relationships of love impaired. The insensitivity of many Lagos parents to the emotional problems of childhood will tend, too, to drive the problems deeper. Such emotional insecurity may make it difficult for a couple to commit their feelings to each other, or to overcome conflicts in marriage. At the same time, the exchange of children between members of the family encourages them to identify themselves with the family group, and they must learn not to rely too much on any one relationship. It is arguable that they grow up to depend less emotionally on any single attachment. The experiences of childhood prepare them against the uncertainties of marriage: failure causes less suffering, if feelings are not deeply involved. But by learning to trust rather in the solidarity of the family group, they limit the intensity of their feelings.

There seems, then, to be a parallel between the ways in which emotional and economic insecurity influence marriage. Just as the uncertainty of a husband's ability or willingness to provide always for his wife may lead her to protect herself by an independent income and the support of her family group, so the uncertainty of individual attachments may lead both men and women to be wary of emotional dependence on any one person, and so trust rather to the strength of family loyalties. And just as companionship in marriage becomes more possible with economic

[1] See for instance John Bowlby, *Child Care and the Growth of Love.*

security, so the more intimate and continuous the relationship
between parents and children, the more likely that children will
grow up to look for a similar relationship in marriage.

In this discussion of some Lagos families, I have tried to
bring out a theme which seems especially relevant to the evolution of urban patterns of life. In any society, people look for
secure affection above all to their family relationships, and find
there also much practical help. Without this fundamental assur-
ance, they tend to lack confidence in other social roles. The
stability of family relationships is therefore very important, but
the emphasis varies according to whether ties of marriage or
ties of blood command the strongest loyalties. Traditionally, in
Nigerian societies, the households of husbands and wives were
subordinate to a wider family grouping. But as this subordination
was not questioned, and the family group shared a common
dwelling, obligations of marriage and of kinship could, at least
in principle, be reconciled within the values of the culture. In
Lagos, as households tend more and more to live apart, the group
reasserts its common interests by frequent meetings both formal
and informal, by the acceptance of mutual obligations, and by
caring for each other's children. But this pattern of family
affairs does not seem to have reasserted so effectively the authority
of the group over relationships between husband and wife, nor
is the group so responsible for the women who have married
into it. If wives have more freedom from the control of their
husbands' family, they cannot at the same time depend on them
so much. But they cannot instead depend more on their husbands,
unless he can both ensure their welfare, and reconcile his obligations to her with those to his kin. She, for her part, may put more
trust in an economic independence, and the support her own
family can give her. So the dispersal of the family group is not
necessarily compensated by the strengthening of ties of marriage.
In a time of rapid social change, people may rely less on any
relationship, and as this also affects the care of children, the next
generation may grow up without the experience of secure attachments, and so less able to form them.

The reconciliation of ties of marriage and kinship seems a
crucial issue in the evolution of Lagos family life, and the conflict of interest becomes especially clear when people are faced

F

with a sudden change in their circumstances. Slum clearance tended to bring into the open latent divergences in patterns of life. But before discussing how the lives of the people of central Lagos changed when they were moved, it is necessary to say something about their economic circumstances. The way in which these were affected profoundly influenced their social situation.

6

THE ECONOMY OF CENTRAL
LAGOS

LAGOS is the principal port of Nigeria, and the slum clearance area lies at the heart of its commercial life, between the two main streets of shops. The neighbourhood is surrounded by the largest markets in cloth, vegetables, meat and poultry, enamel and earthenware, herbs, fancy goods and fruit; and is within a few minutes walk of the great importing houses. Much of the working population of Lagos passes every day by its narrow lanes. The people of the neighbourhood earn their living from the commerce of the city. Most of the men are traders, importers and exporters, shop keepers, dockers and market porters; drivers, watchmen, clerks or mechanics for the foreign firms, or craftsmen who often deal in goods on the side— bicycle repairers selling second-hand machines and tyres, spray painters selling paint, blacksmiths buying up used tins and making them into cheap oil-lamps. The women nearly all trade.

OCCUPATIONS

The occupations of the larger sample interviewed are set out in Table IV. The proportion of men in business or trade is markedly greater than for Lagos as a whole. No figures are available for an exact comparison, but a census of Lagos taken in 1950 lists only 10% of men in occupations which are here classified as trading or business—a difference of nearly 20%.[1]

Women, throughout the township, are predominantly traders. In the census 77% of working women are engaged in trade, somewhat less than in the larger sample in central Lagos. But

[1] The other differences are relatively slight; the proportion of clerks in my sample is only 4–5% higher, and of skilled manual workers about the same as in the census. There are fewer in the professions or not working at all, and no farmers or public service workers such as soldiers and police, each of which group accounts for 3% of the occupations of the men of the township.

TABLE IV[1]

OCCUPATIONS

(Percentages of 201 men and 171 women
interviewed in central Lagos.)

	Men	Women
Clerical	18%	1%
Skilled manual	30%	2%
Labouring	13%	—
Trading	26%	87%
Business	3%	—
Professional	2%	1%
Native doctors and priests	3%	1%
Not working	5%	8%

the striking difference is in the proportion not working at all—
42% of all women in Lagos township in 1950, compared with
only 8% of the women interviewed in the two samples, and 5% of
the wives in the households of the men interviewed. The contrast
is probably not as great as these figures suggest: many married
women living with their husbands may not have bothered to
mention their own occupations when enumerated in the census,
and the large number returned as 'home makers' no doubt often
traded as well. But it is also true that the unique advantages of
central Lagos enable many women to earn an income from petty
trading which they could not secure elsewhere in the township,
and alternative occupations for women are few.

The people of central Lagos are, therefore, largely dependent

[1] The larger sample, being a random selection of individuals, has roughly equal
numbers of men and women, and can therefore represent more accurately the
occupations of women than the smaller sample, since most heads of households
were men. The occupations of men householders distribute very similarly to those
of the men in the larger sample: there are relatively more in business, and correspondingly fewer traders, but the distinction between these occupations is rather
arbitrary. Business men include principally contractors, the owner of a printing
press, and a few importers and exporters whom I have distinguished from traders
because their affairs are conducted on rather different lines.

Native doctors and priests include a number of Arabic teachers, who earn their
living partly by writing charms and spells. The client is provided with a text from
the Koran appropriate to his problem, on a piece of paper or a slate: he either
swallows the paper, or washes the ink off the slate and drinks it, so incorporating
the virtue of the text.

upon being at the centre of commerce for their livelihood. Traders and many of the craftsmen work on their own account, and depend for their livelihood on attracting a group of regular customers who live or work nearby, and to whom they are readily available. In the sample of householders, all the traders and businessmen, and half the skilled manual workers were self-employed. Even some of the labourers worked independently as market porters. In all, only 40% of those at work earned a wage, and many of these traded on the side. An assistant in a Syrian textile shop, for instance, also dealt in Nigerian tobacco; a sanitary inspector in second-hand bicycle parts; a post office clerk in poultry. Men whose terms of employment do not permit them any other gainful occupation often start businesses in their wife's name—and are occasionally cheated, when she interprets a legal fiction to her own advantage, and deserts with the profits. Most men prefer to be independent, and clerical workers in government and commerce, who have gained experience and earn enough to save, tend to retire early and try their luck as traders. Apart from the attraction of being one's own master, the rewards may be greater too. In the sample of householders, the average income of the self-employed men was more than double that of the wage-earners. The advantage lies chiefly with the successful trader or contractor; the independent craftsman earned only about 30s. a month more on average than the skilled employees.

INCOMES

The shabbiness of the houses of central Lagos disguises how widely the residents vary in prosperity. Only the chrome-tipped fin of a Pontiac, edged into the angle of a lane, may distinguish the home of a business man with a profit of several thousand pounds a year from that of his neighbour, who earns perhaps £200 as a carpenter for the railways. A woman who shares two small rooms with her daughter and several grandchildren may be hawking loaves of bread for a few pounds a month; but equally, she may be using her shabby parlour as an office from which she runs a valuable export business in hand-woven cloth. Wealth is stored in boxes of clothes and jewellery, or invested in a son at Manchester University, a daughter learning nursing at a London hospital, or in the pious distinction of having made the pilgrimage to Mecca. Rich and poor live side by side, in the same crowded quarters. In one house, for instance, the head of one household made about six thousand a year, and another seven pounds a month: a casual visitor would not have recognised which was which.

In both the samples interviewed, the income of men and women ranged from less than £6 a month to more than £40. It is difficult to assess incomes at all accurately, especially when they depend on profits which may vary from month to month. But at least in the interviews with household heads, the estimates followed thorough discussion. Where income varied, an average profit was assessed. Gifts and allowances, whether regular or irregular, were excluded, and the figures given below are based only on earnings, profits and rents.

TABLE V

INCOME

(Percentages of 85 men and 25 women householders[1]
in central Lagos.)

Monthly income	Men	Women
£0 –£5	7%	20%
£6 –£10	26%	28%
£11–£20	36%	40%
£21–£30	19%	4%
£31–£40	2%	4%
£41+	9%	4%
Not given	1%	—

In all occupations there is a wide range of income, except for labourers, who seldom earned more than £10 a month. The

[1] Heads of households might be expected to earn rather more than the general population of residents of central Lagos, since they exclude young single men just starting on a career, and wives dependent on their husbands. But for men, there is little difference: the figures above correspond within a few per cent to those for the larger sample. The two samples of women vary more: while in both the proportion earning over £20 a month is the same, the percentage of women in the larger sample earning £11–£20 is only 23%, and correspondingly more earn less than £11 and less than £6.

The Economy of Central Lagos

median monthly incomes[1] of men householders in different kinds of occupation is as follows:

Labourers	£7
Employed skilled manual workers	£14½
Self-employed skilled manual workers	£15
Clerks	£18
Traders and businessmen	£20

The figures for labourers would be even lower, but for one or two men who also worked as tailors or traders in their spare time. The mean incomes are somewhat higher, and for traders and businessmen very much higher—over £51, as the average is inflated by one or two outstandingly successful men. The median income of women householders, excluding gifts and allowances, was £10, and of the wives of household heads living with them, £6. Here again, the mean is much higher than the median—nearly double—because of the outstanding prosperity of a few women traders.

No comparable surveys of incomes have yet been made for Lagos as a whole. But since traders and business men earn the most, and there are three times as many of them as in all Lagos, the slum clearance area is probably one of the most prosperous communities in the town—especially as so many of the women are able to make a worth-while profit from dressmaking or trade. Unlike many European cities, the successful have not deserted the old quarters. Their prosperity depends too much upon being at the centre of commerce. It is founded on the accessibility of the neighbourhood to both local and up-country customers, upon relationships of trust and convenience elaborated over many years, and habits of trade which become in time as valuable as the circumstances which gave rise to them. The prosperity of central Lagos is, therefore, extremely vulnerable to any disturbance in its familiar pattern.

---

[1] When a group of figures are placed in order from lowest to highest, the median is the figure in the middle of the series: that is, if the median income of a group of labourers is £7, half earn more and half less than this. When incomes vary greatly, the median represents the income of the group better than the mean (which is the sum of a group of figures divided by the number of figures in the group).

THE PATTERN OF TRADE

The traders buy their goods almost entirely from the shops and markets of central Lagos. A few bring produce by canoe down the creek from Badagri, or have a relative in the country who rails them supplies—but these were only a tenth of the traders interviewed.

Since both shops and markets are near at hand, it costs little in porterage to carry a stock of goods home. Many of the stall-holders bring their goods home with them every night to save the cost of a watchman. Much of the selling is done at home too, even by those who rent a market stall. This is an important advantage of trading as a livelihood for a wife. She can trade and do her housework at the same time. She need keep no hours; her customers know where to find her at any time. Often when I was interviewing in the evenings, a little girl would come into the yard for a few pennyworth of beans for her mother, or a woman stopped to appraise a length of cloth. About half the traders interviewed, especially the women, sold only at home, and a further 20% also hawked their wares. Apart from 3% who took their goods outside Lagos for sale, the rest had a shop or stall—in a market or a street—though they would not, of course, refuse a customer who came to the house. The tenants traded as much from their homes as the owners, usually squatting outside by the street entrance, where they could display their wares.

So many women can trade profitably from their own door-steps only because the centre of Lagos attracts a daily throng of people from outside the neighbourhood—both from elsewhere in the township, and inland. As one woman said, 'It's the natural beauty of Lagos—I mean, as a port and commercial centre. They refuse an article for two shillings in Ibadan, saying they can get it for one and sixpence in Lagos. Even when they find it costs them half-a-crown in Lagos they are not undeceived—it must be better.' Some of the traders are themselves wholesalers, dealing with market women from Abeokuta or Ibadan. Others are selling to foreigners, or dispatching their goods overseas. But many depend simply on attracting a few shillings from the stream of people who pass along the lanes every day; they sell cigarettes, matches, cola nuts, friend plantains and Coca Cola to office workers, snacks to schoolchildren, bowls of soup. And the residents are, of course, trading amongst themselves, preparing beans or flour cakes in their backyards for the neighbouring housewives. The less well-established women traders hawk their goods about the streets, and work hardest for least profit.

But most of the traders do not depend only on casual custom. They also have regular customers whom they can trust, and to whom they extend credit. Because of this they can keep them against competition. A seller of bread or cooked food, for instance, will go to the office where her regular customers work at the end of the month, and collect what is due to her when they are paid. A cloth seller can charge a much higher margin of profit if she allows the customer a month to pay. The maxim, 'no credit, no trade' was often repeated to me, and it is this willingness to trust people whom you know, together with the central position of the neighbourhood, and the accessibility of the traders at all hours in their own homes which enables them to acquire and keep their own group of customers.

Most traders specialise in a particular article or category of goods, with which they are familiar. Girls learn a trade from the women of their household: they serve at the stalls after school, and watch the business when their mother or aunt is called away. 'They each have their small tray, and they follow their mother. If she is going out, they cry if they are not allowed to go with her— and if she is not going, then they go on their own,' as one father remarked. Sometimes girls inherit their mother's trade, and continue to serve the same customers. They grow up with the bustle of trade, from their babyhood when they crawled amongst the bales of cloth in their mother's market stall, to their old age when, even in retirement, they will sit over a dusty tray of rusting tins, 'just so as not to be sitting for nothing'. Trading becomes second nature, and they know by heart the techniques of the market. Men, too, sometimes take up a trade in which relatives are already established. But others merely consult their friends, and try their luck in a promising line with whatever capital they can raise.

A quarter of both men and women traders dealt in textiles or clothes. It can be the most profitable of lines, but needs knowledge of the styles in demand, and where to place them. Most traders, therefore, specialise in particular styles or materials, or cater for a special market.[1] One man I interviewed made a good living buying Yoruba styles of prints in Lagos, where most of them are landed, and selling them to Yoruba in the Eastern Region. In Port Harcourt he bought styles popular amongst Ibo for sale to their countrymen in Lagos. He travelled by air at times to attend to urgent orders. A woman who specialised in hand-woven Nigerian cloth showed me a file of telegrams from Accra, Monrovia and Freetown placing orders and reporting on the state of the market. She worked entirely from her own home, where she used to sell to crews from the ships who knew her address. Her profit was more than £100 a month. But most of the cloth sellers earn much less, some merely hawking a few lengths made up into head-ties for a profit of £2 to £3 a month.

Clothes and textiles seem to be the only articles in which men and women trade in equal proportion, and they generally handle different aspects. The woman who dealt in hand-woven cloth, for instance, had trained her daughter rather than her son to the business, because, 'it's not a trade a boy can handle'. Women usually deal in lengths of cloth, men in made-up articles. For the rest, men deal in a great variety of goods. Some do not specialise in any line, but speculate on whatever seems to be in demand. Others, like the Hausa traders in leather work and carving, depend mostly on foreign customers. The women, however,

---

[1] Cloth seems always to have been prominent amongst Lagos imports, and special designs are manufactured for the Lagos market in Lancashire, Holland and Japan. Writing 150 years ago, Captain Adams' list of recommended articles of trade itemizes several dozen kinds of cloth: his other suggestions are by comparison perfunctory. The list is as follows:

Blue bafts	Hair romals	Lungee	Gunpowder
Bejutapauts—	Red Dane romal	handerchiefs	Guns
blue and red	Allijars	Pullical	Tobacco
Chelloe	Sastracundies	handkerchiefs	Salt
Niccanee	Cadawapores	Silesias	Iron
Photaes	White bafts	Half says	Lead bars
Tapsail	(or gurrahs)	Green and	Brass pans
Neganipauts	Hoo Hoos	yellow ells	Neptunes
Abba Photae or	Chollets	Moor blue cloth	Bottles
Tom Coffee romal	Chintz	Blue baize	Cowries
Bonny blue romal	Guinea stuff	Worsted caps	Beads
Tape romal	Taffity	Hats	Hardware
Abang romal	Cuttence	Spirits	Earthenware
Quaducker romal	Sarry	Rum	
Ashantee romal	Bandanna	French brandy	

deal predominantly in three kinds of trade only: cloth, provisions, and foodstuffs.

TABLE VI

WHAT TRADERS SELL

(Proportions of 51 men and 149 women traders interviewed in central Lagos.)

	Men	Women
Textiles	25%	24%
Provisions and Cigarettes	4%	23%
Foodstuffs	12%	31%
Other	43%	18%
No speciality	16%	4%

The men who engage in the characteristically women's trades—foodstuffs or provisions—are usually selling in bulk, wholesale.

The streets display a greater variety of wares than the markets, where traders in a particular article tend to congregate together, but in one of the large markets of Lagos Island my research assistant counted eighty poultry sellers, sixteen butchers, ninety-nine dealers in imported cloth, twenty in head-ties, four each in second-hand clothes and haberdashery, eighty-four in native cloth, five in caps, six in shoes, twenty-three in beads and gold ornaments, 159 in herbs and medicines, thirteen in cooked foods, sixty-five in garri, vegetables and rice, thirteen in cola nuts, thirty-one in crockery and cutlery, six in pots, baskets, trays and calabashes, seventeen in mats, two in suitcases, three in skins, five in sacks, and one each in tyres, soap, rope, snuff, firewood and sponges. There were also four hairdressers and three tailors: five stalls were used as stores and thirteen were vacant. Of these almost 700 stall-holders, five-sixths were women.[1]

Articles of trade are not equally profitable. Amongst the traders interviewed in the general sample from central Lagos, the proportion of cloth sellers earning £11 or more a month was double that of food and provision sellers. Those who did not specialise at all made most: the majority had incomes over £20 a

[1] Two years later, this market had almost doubled in size.

75

month. Probably only those with substantial capital in the first place can afford to speculate in this way—few women do it. But in general, income seems to depend more upon the capital invested than the kind of stock, and because they usually had less capital, women traders made less than the men. Two thirds of them earned less than £11 a month, as against a quarter of the men, while only 14% compared with 38% earned upwards of £21. But even when they made no more than a few pounds a month, the money was still an important contribution to the household economy. It is certainly untrue, as is sometimes suggested, that women trade more from force of habit than for profit, and often sell without any worthwhile return.[1]

It has also been suggested that such widespread petty trading, even if viable, harms the Nigerian economy: so many middlemen must raise the price to the consumer, and divert manpower from more productive work. This view is examined and rejected by P. T. Bauer in his controversial book *West African Trade*. He argues that trade is extremely competitive, and if there were means to cut out some of the middlemen and undersell them, the opportunity would have been taken. In any case, there is no more directly productive work available for the traders to turn to. This pattern of trade is itself much more productive than is often recognised: it stimulates the exploitation of resources, ensures that nothing of any value—packing cases, old tins, bottles, paper— goes to waste, and distributes goods through a vast territory where transport facilities are inadequate. The ramification of small dealers compensates for the shortage of capital: by breaking bulk, they bring goods to the consumer in a quantity he can afford.

Even the larger traders seldom have much capital available in cash, their chief asset being their access to short-term credit. So most stocks must be disposed of quickly, and the elaborate organisation of middlemen provides an efficient and sensitive means of distributing them in a discriminating and competitive market. For example, a carpenter I interviewed also dealt in sugar, cement, bicycles, iron sheets. When one of the big importing firms landed a cargo of, say, sugar, it would be bought up by wholesalers able to acquire large stocks on credit. These wholesalers would then get in touch with him, and he might take

[1] For a fuller account of women's trades see S. Comhaire-Sylvain, 'Le Travail des Femmes a Lagos, Nigeria'.

£1,000 of sugar against a deposit of £200. He then sold in turn to smaller dealers, who were not in a position to deal on credit. He would distribute his stock amongst ten or so, each taking £50 to £100 worth. Some of these would retail to the public, others to petty traders. So the sugar passed through four or five hands. His own profit would be about £150. This chain of distribution could only be shortened if there were more dealers with warehouses and shops, who could afford to keep their capital tied up in unsold stock for a longer time: and Nigeria has not yet reached this stage of capital accumulation.

The dealers also save their customers time and trouble. A family in a village near Ibadan chooses a cloth for some celebration. A petty trader carries their order to the Ibadan market. The market woman then comes to Lagos for it, buying from a stall holder who will have obtained it, directly or through an intermediary from the importers. The traders make short journeys, fulfilling several orders at a time, know where to find what they want, and can buy on cash or credit the quantity they need. They can bring the cloth to the family more efficiently than the family could fetch it for themselves, saving them a journey which is expensive, takes them from their work, and at the end of which they would not be able to find what they wanted on such favourable terms.

The importer with a turnover of £80,000 a year, and the hawker with a few odd remnants of cloth are the two ends of a chain whereby goods are passed to the consumer, without requiring at any stage the accumulation of capital which in Nigeria is scarce. The residents of central Lagos are very well placed to exploit this pattern of trade. It provides the housewife with a profitable occupation which she can reconcile with her housework and the care of her children; and gives her the independence which she needs to protect herself in marriage, and to contribute to the welfare of her family group.

EXPENDITURE

The prosperity of central Lagos is, however, only relative. A few of the most successful traders and businessmen are able to buy property or save, but most people can barely manage to live within their incomes. Men will talk hopefully of amassing a small capital, and retiring to their home town to build a house and open a shop, but in practice, any increase in their earnings tends to be absorbed at once by new family responsibilities. They have more dependants, or if they are well-off, they may undertake the further education of their children. They have very little protection against a slump in their earnings.

The cost of living in Lagos is, besides, the highest in Nigeria. Little food is grown locally, and prices in the market are higher than in most other towns. The householders interviewed spent on average £9 a month on food, drink, and cooking fuel, which works out at £1 17*s.* for each member of the household. For the men, this amounted to about half their incomes.[1] Excluding five who were spending more than their current income at the time of interview—because of unemployment or a slump in trade—the figure is a few per cent less. The largest number spent 40% to 50% of their income on food, but the proportion ranged widely from four who spent less than 20%, to ten who spent over 80%. The relative size of the housekeeping budget depended more on the size of income than the number of mouths to feed: those who earned over £20 a month spent an average of 34%, while those earning less than £10 spent almost 70% of their income on food, but the largest households only spent 9% more than the smallest. The amounts spent by the women householders were similar, but they cannot usefully be presented as a proportion of their incomes, since they often lived on irregular gifts, allowances from husbands or children, or savings, as much as on what they earned.

Besides an allowance for housekeeping, 71% of the married men also gave their wives a personal allowance, and sometimes a few pence pocket money to their children. As a whole, these allowances average £3 6*s.*, including grants for rent and living expenses of wives outside the household, and occasionally for the maintenance of children with a grandparent. Most husbands also spend a good deal of money on clothes for their wives and children, particularly at festival times: a clerk, earning £34 a month, spent £40 on clothes for his family at Christmas, and about £25 at Easter—'At Easter it can't be so much, just small,

---

[1] In calculating expenditure as a proportion of income, regular allowances from relatives have been added to the income, but not irregular gifts. Only one or two men received such regular allowances.

small. If we spend too much like that we shall fall.' A prosperous woman trader bought complete outfits for her children at the principal Muslim festivals. She estimated the cost at £30 to £40, but her daughter protested, 'Why! Last time the trinkets she bought me alone cost about £30, and she buys the most expensive cloth.' Clothes, rather than furniture or household equipment, seem the most generally accepted way of spending money for show, at least amongst the Yoruba.

Apart from housekeeping, and allowances to dependents, the largest item of regular recurrent expenditure was rents. The average rent paid by tenants, excluding electric light, and 'conservancy' (the collection of sewage), where these were charged separately, was two pounds monthly—£1 16s. 7d. a room. For most of the men who were tenants, this represented between 5% and 20% of their income—14% on average. These figures are certainly below the average for the township as a whole. An enquiry by the Federal Department of Statistics in January 1959 found the average rent paid by one-room households in the previous month to be £2 14s. Their survey covered a sample of all houses in Lagos except the suburbs of Ikoyi, where the expatriate officials have their expensive homes. They do not compare rents with the incomes of tenants, but a previous survey by the Department in 1951, amongst clerks and employed manual workers, showed that the proportion of earnings paid in rent rose from 15% for tenants earning £15 to 27% for those earning £5. As a whole, therefore, they were paying relatively more for their accommodation than the tenants amongst the householders interviewed. A more direct comparison can be made with the households interviewed by my research assistant in a block of houses in the back streets of Ebute Metta. The standard of accommodation was certainly no higher than in central Lagos; the neighbourhood was far less convenient, at the end of an unmade road ten minutes from the nearest bus stop; and the residents earned less. Yet the average rents were 18s. a month higher than in central Lagos: over two-thirds of the tenants paid more than £2 a month, compared with only half in central Lagos, where there were, also, many more owner-occupiers paying no rent at all.

Rents are low in the centre of the town only because the tenants are long established. Though the houses are often in poor repair, without piped water or sewage, accommodation is much sought after because it is convenient, and often no worse than much of the suburbs. The buildings are more substantial than in many neighbourhoods on the outskirts of the town, where villages have been overtaken by expansion. But an established tenant can resist for a while a general rise in rents. He cannot be summarily evicted, and if his landlord shares the same house with him, they are likely to be on friendly terms, and he can expect some consideration. Amongst the householders interviewed in central Lagos, 65% of the tenants who had been eleven or more years in residence paid less than £2 rent a month. But of those who had held their tenancies for less than eleven years only 38% paid as little. Since rents in Lagos rise alarmingly every year, under the pressure of a continually growing population, an established tenancy is a valuable asset.

The householders were not asked for a detailed budget in the interviews. Apart from housekeeping, personal allowances and rent, they spent most on the gifts to relatives described in an earlier chapter, on clothes, and celebrations. About a fifth of them spent altogether more than £20 a month, two-fifths between £11 and £20, and the remaining two-fifths £10 or less. For 15% their expenditure was greater than their income. They made up the balance partly from loans or savings, and sometimes by help from other members of the household.

In comparing the expenditure of the households with income, I have considered only the income of the household head, from earnings, profits, rents or regular gifts from relatives. Even when other members of the household were earning, the head did not expect them to contribute towards their board: children usually begin to support their parents only after they leave their household. There was only one instance of a son still living in his father's household contributing to it: he paid over his entire wage, but this was partly because his father had undertaken the whole cost of his forthcoming marriage. But though the household heads did not expect the other members to pay a regular part of the expenses, they often depended on their voluntary help in difficulties—mostly from their wives. When expenditure exceeded income, this was often because the husband did not, in fact, manage to meet the figure he estimated as his monthly housekeeping allowance. His wife or wives, with good or bad grace, had little choice but to make up the balance. As one husband confessed, 'Sometimes I haven't a penny to put down for food. When she asks me for food money as I'm going off to work, I just have to tell her I can't make ends meet. If she makes a scene I clear out. But when I get home in the afternoon, I find my dinner ready. My wife's a good child.' A schoolteacher said 'For all my expenditure, I depend very much on my wife. Even at the end of the month I depend on her, and she gives me freely, up to ten pounds a month.' So although husbands do not claim any right to a share of their wives' earnings, many households would be seriously in debt without their help. Otherwise they have to depend on loans from friends, credit, or gifts from other members of their family: but although young men turn readily to an older brother or their parents for a casual loan, more senior members of the family feel a little humiliated at having to appeal to relatives for their everyday expenses. They prefer to settle their financial problems inside the household.

This review of the income and expenditure of families in central Lagos shows in how many ways they depend upon the neighbourhood in which they lived. There were few professional men or senior clerks in the community: its property rested on the relatively high proportion of traders, businessmen and self-employed craftsmen, who owed their livelihood to being at the centre of the city's commerce. Even the labourers were sometimes able to eke out the low wages paid in Lagos for unskilled work with part-time trading or tailoring. Nearly all the wives were trading—some very profitably—and their earnings were a very important reserve from which to meet up the expenses of the household. Old people depended upon rents from property in the neighbourhood, or on living amongst their kin, who supported them and provided them with a home. But also, because of the community in which they lived, their expenses were relatively low. A third lived in houses owned by themselves or their relatives, and the tenants, being long established, paid less rent than in other parts of Lagos. Most, too, lived within easy walking distance of their work, their relatives, their social activities, and had little to pay in fares. Slum clearance, therefore, seemed likely to involve a radical reorganization of their economic affairs.

G

7

THE SLUM CLEARANCE SCHEME

THE standard of housing in Lagos is low. Most houses have neither piped water nor a sewage system. The only bathroom or lavatory may be a rough shelter of corrugated iron with a bucket, knocked together in a corner of the yard. Water has to be collected from a stand-pipe in the street, and latrine buckets collected by a service of the Town Council. There is no water-born sewage system for the city. In central Lagos the drains are open, often a shallow channel running down the middle of the lane, in which refuse and ordure float. In wet weather the drains overflow. In the older parts of the town, the houses are mostly of brick and concrete, with corrugated sheeting on the roof, but extensions of unlined weatherboard or iron have often been built onto them. The houses are poorly maintained, and within the slum clearance area they have deteriorated the more because improvements which would increase their value are prohibited. On the mainland, speculative builders have put up trade houses—large two-storey buildings, with lines of rooms opening off a corridor on each floor: they may contain two dozen tenant families, without any facilities for cooking or washing, apart from a small yard with a lavatory shed. On the outskirts of Lagos, beyond the township boundary, much of the building is in impermanent materials, and the roads are unmade. Apart from the suburbs where expatriates live, every part of Lagos is congested. In the four streets studied there were 3·5 people to a room, and most of these rooms were small, dark and poorly ventilated.

Apart from their inconvenience, such living conditions may do serious harm to the health of the people of Lagos. The commonest serious illnesses in the city are infective and parasitic diseases, expecially malaria; bronchitis and pneumonia; dysentery and diarrhoea; and skin complaints. The first three groups caused nearly half the deaths registered in 1947. These are all diseases likely to be aggravated or to spread more easily through dirt and overcrowding. The annual report of the Federal Medical Services for 1957 remarks, 'The eradication, or diminution, of pneumonia and dysentery as causes of death are long-term projects, involving such social advances as slum clearance, better housing, waterborn sewage and, not least important, the education of the public in the proper use of these amenities . . .' The report comments a few pages later, 'The slum clearance scheme of the Lagos Executive Development Board, which is steadily going ahead, has not yet made any appreciable impact on many areas where living conditions generally, and the standards of environ-mental hygiene in particular, remained of a very low order. The array of street traders scattering litter, the lack of adequate kitchen and latrine accommodation in many of the houses, and the limited number of public dustbins—all contribute towards the existing unsatisfactory and in some cases appalling state of many side streets and alleys.'[1] Apart from diseases, the congested streets probably also contributed to the number of accidents, which were responsible for more hospital admissions than any disease group.

The need to improve health is urgent, and above all amongst children. Almost 60% of the deaths recorded in 1958 were of children under five. Amongst these children the death rate is about 60 per thousand—more than ten times the rate, for instance, in the County of London. The rate is roughly seven times as high as in London for children between five and fourteen, three times as high between fifteen and twenty-four, and twice between twenty-five and forty-four. Since the correlation of housing with health has not been studied in Lagos, it is not possible to assess how far bad housing, rather than unbalanced diet, inadequate medical facilities, and lack of public knowledge, is responsible for ill-health. Both the death rate and mortality rate are nearly three times higher on the island than the mainland: but this is probably because the general hospital and maternity hospital are on the island, and because there is more waste land on the

[1] Annual Report on the Medical Services of the Federal Territory of Lagos for the year 1957, pp. 25 and 27. The report for 1958 comments, 'The general pattern of mortality shows no change. The main killers are still pneumonia, malaria and dysentery, and these three account for nearly half the deaths in Lagos.' p. 25.

mainland where the dead can be buried without notification (a burial permit for an authorised cemetery can only be obtained on presenting a death certificate). It has been noticed that tuberculosis patients often live in particularly insanitary homes, but this seems to be a consequence rather than a cause of their illness. However, though the influence of housing has not been determined, health is clearly the most compelling reason for a radical housing policy.

On grounds of health alone, the Lagos Executive Development Board might not have undertaken the clearance of central Lagos as its first object. Other neighbourhoods, where housing is as bad or worse, would have presented fewer difficulties. But it became clear soon after the war that Lagos would become, within a few years, the federal capital of an independent Nigeria, and the obtrusive shabbiness of central Lagos began to attract attention as an affront to the dignity of the future capital. It was also the area in which traffic congestion was most acute. It will be argued later that the decision to begin with central Lagos was mistaken, but certainly on grounds of health, traffic congestion, and national pride, it seemed an obvious choice.

The Lagos slum clearance scheme was put into effect in 1955. It was to involve the rehousing of about 200,000 people over a period of five to seven years. 'The scope of the scheme comprises the clearance and redevelopment of seventy acres of built-up land bounded approximately by Broad Street, Balogun Street and Victoria Street, together with an area to the east of Victoria Street. Streets will be widened to meet the increased traffic demands and, at the same time, rear access service roads to the commercial premises fronting these main streets will be provided. Of the total area developed there will be available twenty nett acres of residential development and twenty-two nett acres of commercial development.'[1] The L.E.D.B. was to provide roads, water, electricity and drains, but not itself rebuild: nor, in spite of the Board's recommendation, did the government allow funds for a piped sewage system.

This scheme differs in two very important respects from the development undertaken before the war. Firstly, to meet the objections of the families who owned the freehold of the land—

[1] Lagos Executive Development Board, Annual Report and Accounts (1958–59), p. 17.

who were protesting that they were to lose their birthright, and that the most valuable sites in Lagos would pass into the hands of alien commercial firms—the owners were promised that the plots would be re-allotted to them. To enable them to repurchase their land, part of the cost of redevelopment would be met from public funds. The owners themselves were to bear a rate assessed at 20% of the compensation paid for each plot when it was vested in the Board. So, where for instance the owner of a house had received £1,000 in compensation when he was dispossessed, he would be offered a freehold of a redevelopment plot in the area, if it were of the same size, for £1,200. The new plots, however, would generally be rather larger than the old, so an owner might in fact be required to pay more than 20% above the compensation he had received, to cover the difference between the size of his original plot and the new one allotted to him. He had then to find the money to rebuild his house. But clearly, even if they could afford it, only about half the original owners could be given this opportunity to return, since each plot was to be larger, and streets widened. The remainder could buy freeholds in estates which the Board was developing elsewhere in Lagos.

Secondly, the Board accepted the responsibility to rehouse those who had to be moved. They built a housing estate at Suru Lere, on the outskirts of the township, where terraced cottages of one to four rooms were provided at a subsidised rent of twenty-five shillings a room a month. This estate was planned to house the former residents of central Lagos only temporarily: after eighteen months, the plots in the cleared area would be ready for reconveyance, the original owners would return there, and houses on the estate would be available to receive those to be moved under the next phase of the scheme. It would, of course, have been less cumbersome to move people directly, street by street, from their old homes to the cleared sites as they were rebuilt. But the Board could not do this, since it had promised to allot the land to the former owners as fairly as it could, and without this promise, the scheme would never have been approved. They seem to have expected that most of the former tenants in central Lagos would also return there, or like the owner for whom plots would not be available after redevelopment, establish themselves permanently elsewhere.

Suru Lere means in Yoruba, 'patience is rewarded'. To help

residents bear more easily their temporary evacuation to the suburbs, £200,000 were set aside to compensate traders whose profits suffered, landlords dependent on rents from property which had been pulled down, and other cases of hardship, at the Board's discretion. The Board also undertook to provide transport for the move to the rehousing estate, and back to central Lagos, at their own expense.

The scheme came into operation in the autumn of 1955, in the face of vehement protests from many of the residents, especially the owners. An association of the residents of central Lagos was formed to organise protests, and put their grievances before the Board. In June, 1956, the Chief Executive Officer of the L.E.D.B. prepared a list of these objections, setting against each the re-assurances provided by the scheme, which was published both in newspapers and on posters. The list recognises twenty-two objections, ranging from the demolishing of three mosques to the fear that all old people were to be sent to an asylum. But the fundamental objections concerned two points. Firstly, that residents were not covered against the hardships of moving, especially loss of business premises and profits, and the cost of rents on the rehousing estate. To this the Board replied that temporary premises would be provided for African business men in central Lagos, and that funds were available to deal with genuine cases of hardship 'sympathetically but not extravagantly'; it pointed out that rents on the rehousing estate, at 25s. a room, were subsidised. Secondly, and most important, were the objections that owners would not be able to return to central Lagos, either because land would be restricted, or because they could not afford it. The Board replied that all land would as far as possible be reconveyed to the original owner; and where this was not possible, he would be offered an equivalent area nearby, or—if this too was impossible—he would be given, 'priority claim to any land within the cleared area not taken up by an original owner, or if no such land available, priority consideration to any other freehold land that the Board has developed.' On the questions of the cost of rebuilding, the Board pointed out that the land would be reconveyed at, 'acquired price plus surcharge of only 20%. Federal Government to meet cost of all acquisition of buildings, new roads, road widening, drainage and demolition to the extent of about two million pounds;' that, 'owners may erect single storey or bungalow or ground floor type premises subject to foundations being provided to take two- or three-storey extensions'; and that 95% mortgages were available at 4% interest, without fixed limit.

These answers did not fully answer the objections raised. Although the Board promised to deal sympathetically with cases of hardship, it did not undertake to compensate residents in full for loss of goodwill in their trade, or of rents from property demolished. A fund of £200,000 could not stretch to cover all such losses suffered amongst a population of 200,000 people, where nearly every wife stood to lose an income from petty trading. As to the residents' chances of returning to central Lagos, the Board could only guarantee that every owner of property dispossessed would be offered freehold land to buy somewhere in the township: half of them would, in fact, have to be accommodated outside central Lagos. And in spite of the offer of building loans, it remained exceedingly difficult for the owners to avail themselves of the right to repurchase plots in the cleared areas. In the first place, they had to find 20% more than they had been paid in compensation—more if the new plot was larger. They then had to find the money to build. All houses were to have foundations to take more than one storey, and in the half of the area zoned for commercial use, only the upper floors could be used as accommodation: a family would therefore have to build at least two storeys if they wished to return to central Lagos to live. Regulations required that rooms should not be less than a certain size, the density of occupation should conform to a minimum standard, and the buildings were to be of sound permanent construction. Building costs in Lagos are high, and a house to these standards could not cost less than several thousand pounds. Scarcely any of the owners possessed such capital sums, or were in a position to borrow it. Those who had, preferred to use their capital to expand their business. For these reasons, the safeguards publicized by the Board did not reassure the residents.

The notice setting out the objections to the scheme, and the Board's answers, is dated 27th June, 1956. Early the following morning, a riot broke out when the L.E.D.B. attempted to carry out scheduled demolition in the face of stubborn resistance. The *Daily Times* reported:

The Slum Clearance Scheme

More than two hundred policemen dressed in steel helmets and carrying wicker-work shields and truncheons were yesterday morning drafted to guard the labourers of the Lagos Ex. Dev. Bd. who were employed to demolish a house affected by the slum clearance scheme at Porto Novo Market Street, Lagos.

This followed a disturbance which broke out as a result of resistance by the residents of the house concerned. They refused to leave the premises and refused to allow the workers to carry out demolition work.

Stones were thrown at the first batch of policemen. The situation became more serious when neighbours of the premises joined in the fight and the number of policemen had to be strengthened.

After about an hour, more than half of the demonstrators were dispersed and some of them arrested. One of the residents told the police: 'This is my father's house, and only my dead body can be removed from this place.' He was, however, overpowered and taken into the police van.[1]

The *Daily Service,* which was more sympathetic to the rioters, gave a similar account, but described the fighting in more detail: 'Stones, bottles and sticks were thrown at the police, who in retaliation, used their batons to beat up a number of people, including old women, housewives and mothers with their babies slung to their backs. Many were arrested.'[2]

The L.E.D.B. believed that they could not have carried on without a show of force, and there has been no violence since. But the Residents' Association continued to urge their objections to the scheme. A mass meeting of 'almost a thousand' in February, 1958 passed unanimously fifteen resolutions repeating the familiar protests, and pointed out, 'that it is well over eighteen months since demolition of houses started in central Lagos and up till now not a single building has been put up in the cleared and redeveloped areas. This has brought about great hardships to all displaced landlords and residents, and has created great fears in the minds of all future would-be displaced landlords and residents.' The meeting appealed, 'humbly and respectfully to the Council of Ministers to use their good offices to see that demolition of further houses be suspended until those cleared and redeveloped areas are rebuilt, and residents, shopkeepers displaced are resettled . . . Anyway, the citizens have a right to

[1] *Daily Times,* Lagos, 29th June, 1956.
[2] *Daily Service,* Lagos, 29th June, 1956.

88

ask for sample of what the Government has as benefit for them in pursuing this scheme.' A memorandum to the L.E.D.B. in October sets out three reasons why owners could not afford to rebuild. Compensation did not enable them to meet the reconveyance charges; it might be divided, when the property has been owned in common by a family, some members wishing to repurchase and others not; or it might have been partly used up to pay the rent at Suru Lere and for other living expenses, the owner having no other source of income since the demolition of his property. The memorandum asked for more generous loans and mortgages at lower rates of interest, and permission to build to a higher density of rooms per plot.

In spite of these protests, slum clearance proceeded, and by March, 1959, 6,000 people had been moved. £1,368,696 had been paid in compensation, and nearly £90,000 in awards for hardship. But the problem of how the former owners were to find the means to return had not been solved.[1] The new roads of central Lagos ran between rows of notice boards, announcing the families to whom each plot had been allotted, as if to make clear that the Government, for its part, had fulfilled its promise. But behind the notices, no building was going up. The residents awaiting eviction looked out on acres of vacant lots, where children played football and table tennis, and lines of temporary one-room stalls housed displaced shopkeepers trying to re-establish their custom. Meanwhile, the rehousing estate at Suru Lere had to be expanded, since most of the original tenants were still there. Arrangements were made to add 600 houses to the 900 already built. Patience had not yet had its reward.

The Lagos Executive Development Board was naturally anxious to enable the original owners to rebuild, and to meet cases of hardship, but it was limited by the funds at its disposal. Already by 1958 it was forced to make less generous ex-gratia awards, to conserve its resources. But in urging the scheme

---

[1] In its Report for 1958–59 the L.E.D.B. noted, 'The principal reasons for the delay in rebuilding have been the financial inability of a large number of owners to undertake rebuilding. Discussions have continued throughout the year . . . and the Special Mortgage Fund Scheme . . . was introduced. The Scheme has, however, had limited success because the owners concerned have not considered the money available to them individually, sufficient to assist them in their rebuilding, and representations have been made to the Minister of Lagos Affairs, Mines and Power.' p.18.

forward in spite of these difficulties, it had one very compelling argument. The interests of 200,000 residents should not be allowed to override the will of 35 million Nigerians. Central Lagos was the heart of the Federal capital, and its development was urgent for the sake of national pride. The *Daily Times* had commented severely on the Porto Novo Street riot. 'The spectacle was saddening, and it was bound to arouse the anger of every lover of Nigeria and those who rightly feel that Lagos should, and can, be a worthier capital. It should have occurred to the occupants, and their leaders in particular, that by indulging in foolhardiness, they had only themselves to blame if the police, with Nigeria behind them, got the better of them.'[1] The L.E.D.B. felt not only that Nigeria was behind them, but also that behind the opposition to the scheme were a few men with vested interests in central Lagos, who exploited grievances to their own advantage. Two-thirds of the residents, after all, were tenants, who were to be rehoused in much better accommodation at lower rent. Organised opposition exaggerated the true feelings of the residents, most of whom, they believed, were now fully reconciled to the scheme.

The evidence of the present enquiry suggests that in this the Board were too optimistic. Only three of the householders interviewed, amongst those still living in the clearance area, looked forward to slum clearance with approval. One, a seaman, compared British achievements unfavourably with the parts he had visited in French West Africa. 'It's a trick, they just treat Nigeria as farm . . . In French, they build big houses in city, roads.' Another man already had many close relatives living near the rehousing estate. The third was the wife of an accounts clerk, who in any case planned to join her husband in England in a few months. Eight others were indifferent or undecided. But the remaining ninety-nine were anxious, even despairing. 'You can write down in your report that ever since I heard of the slum clearance, I have been very uneasy in my mind: I wake every morning sick with anxiety,' said a watch repairer whose family owned a small house. And a tenant, an Arabic teacher who had already sent his wives away to their relatives, 'My mind is not at rest at all. I fear it as death. When I think of this removal I can't eat my breakfast.'

[1] *Daily Times,* Lagos, 30th June, 1956.

The Slum Clearance Scheme

Some had already been affected by slum clearance. Landlords had moved from other property already pulled down; traders had watched their profits dwindle, as demolition in the neighbourhood removed their customers; households had scattered anticipating the problems of eviction—'a lame man is not hurt, when war is announced beforehand', as the Yoruba proverb says. And they had already seen how friends and relatives suffered when they had to move. Owners foresaw how compensation might be exhausted in everyday expenses, and the chance of rebuilding lost through divisions in the family.

A member of a large family house described the fate of a cousin, who had gone to Suru Lere from a house he owned in central Lagos: 'First they paid the money to him. Then he was paying £2 10s. rent—he had two rooms at Suru Lere—until the money paid him by the L.E.D.B. was all gone. After a while he is a debtor, and he was told to quit. One brother helped him to his own place at Ebute Metta. But no place for his wife, and his children all scattered: father and mother cannot live together again. When I go to see him there, he always wept. He said, "if it wasn't for my brother, what would I do?" ' My informant added, 'All these notice boards (the notice of the families to whom the plots had been allotted)—I take it to be window-dressing. Just deceiving to show every man has his plot. But who can afford to build? All these buildings going up now are occupied by Syrians. When people come to town, they say they will build this place or that but it is all mouth talk, not heart talk. When he is in his house, he begins to sob.' Most of the owners knew that they would never rebuild in central Lagos. A shopkeeper admitted, 'The charges they are giving us now, I don't think I could afford this area again. I have no thousands of savings. They promise they are going to help us, but they don't give us sufficient money to build a house. We don't know where we are going now.'

Some members of families which owned property feared that once they received compensation in cash, it would either be spent, or divided up. In their view, 'the only remedy is to build another house for us. It is no use giving us compensation: compensation cannot help us. If people are given compensation, some members of the family will want to take their share of the money and the rest will not be enough to build with.' 'We don't want money,' one man protested. 'Let them build a house for us, so that we can be together. We told them from the first, when they began this scheme. Let them build what they want, and let us see first.'

The old people were hardest hit when compensation was divided. They had been used to living in a room of a family house, where their kin could not ignore their welfare. But once the house was pulled down, their own share of the compensation would not provide them with any security, and the family group scattered. For instance, an old man, who was dumb, and lived apart from his wife, shared a room in a family house with a nephew. The family had already received two thousand pounds in compensation, and divided it amongst the five branches which owned the property together. Each branch had in turn subdivided their share, so the old man was only entitled to one or two hundred pounds himself. Since he had no income, this sum could not have kept him for more than a year or two. He was cared for by a niece, who shared the same house, but she—being of the next generation—received only £57. Her livelihood depended on petty trading, and once removed, she did not know where she would find the money to rent a room for her own household, let alone care for her uncle. These practical problems apart, old people are not resilient enough to adapt to a profound disturbance of their way of life. They had their roots in these old houses, almost literally, since it is a custom to bury the afterbirth beneath the house where a child is born. Here were the shrines to their parents, and in the oldest houses, even their graves, dug by tradition within the compound. So there were many stories of old people who had died heartbroken within a few months of their dispossession. A teacher of Arabic, moved from his family home beside the mosque, had gone to the outskirts of Lagos in search of cheap lodging, where he fell sick: 'After five months, willingly or unwillingly, he didn't want to die out there. He had no money, so he managed to walk into town, resting a bit and walking a bit, and he turned up at the mosque, he arrived there late in the evening. He slept in the mosque, and the people used to help him with what they had— but there was no one in a position to accommodate him. He lived in the mosque for five months before he died. A quiet man.'

Though the L.E.D.B. did their best to help these old people, no scheme, however humane, could have avoided such tragedies; grief at a lost home cannot always be appeased by physical welfare and rational arguments for progress. And when they saw the distress of the old people, the land owners of central Lagos were reminded that their own loss meant more to them than merely economic hardship.

These anxieties support the protests put forward by the Residents' Association in their meetings and memoranda. The owners objections were to be expected: they arose from difficulties of which the L.E.D.B. was as well aware as the residents them- selves. But the tenants, too, though they mostly lived in dark cramped rooms without sanitation or running water, the roofs often leaking and the walls begrimed, looked forward to removal with dismay.

They feared the scattering of their households, long journeys and fares they could not afford, isolation and the failure of their own and their wives' trade.

'I can't live there,' a bricklayer protested, speaking of the re- housing estate. 'What about trade of my wives? And if you are not my customer before, how can you come to meet me there? And my old customers, I shall not be able to meet them in time.' He shared a single room at three pounds a month, with two wives, a young daughter and housemaid. A double bed, screened by a curtain, stood against the wall, a single bed against another, a wardrobe piled with china bowls jammed between them. Yet still he saw no attraction in Suru Lere. 'I can't go there. When slum clearance comes now, my senior wife I send to Ilorin, my junior wife to her people's house, my pekin (child) to Ilorin. Myself—I go anywhere I can: no power for me at all again. That's why I don't like to leave this place.'

'I'd be sorry to go for two important things,' a teacher said. 'I work in Lagos, and for all my expenditure I depend very much on my wife. Even at the end of the month I depend on her, and thinking now of my salary, it will be very difficult for me, if I go there, to carry all my responsibilities. My wife would have difficulty in trading out there.'

'It's a matter of busy streets,' explained an electrician, whose wife sold poplins and striped cottons from a pavement stall. 'You look for a market stall in a street where morning and evening people are rushing up and down. At Suru Lere we might be tucked away in some corner. And my wife has to carry her loads from the market morning and evening: it would be impossible to carry them up and down from Suru Lere.'

'My house is no more than eight minutes' walk from the office,' a clerk said, 'but if I move, I shall have to take bus, and my children going to school here too. I'm afraid of this Suru Lere. I went there once—when we were returning, it was a tug of war before we could get a bus. I shall try very hard to get a house in Lagos to remove to instead. I'm thinking about the money I shall be spending daily on transport at Suru Lere. The houses themselves are alright.' Fares would add two or three pounds to his monthly expenses, and travel two hours or more a day.

Because of all these problems, most tenants considered the showers, lavatories and running water that the rehousing estate would provide beside the point. What use were they, if you could not afford to enjoy them?

Their objections were succinctly summarised by a carpenter and dealer, who rented a room at two pounds ten shillings for himself, his two wives, and four children. 'Well,' he said, 'I've no wish to live in Suru Lere, and I pray God to find me some other place. First of all, it'll cause hardship to my children as well as my wives, because they'll have to find transport every day. Secondly, I'll not be able to see my wives' families. Thirdly, most of my people in Porto Novo won't be able to find me when they come to Lagos, and fourthly, all my work is in Lagos. What about my customers who are used to finding me here: am I to wish them goodbye? And then, the condition of the houses at Suru Lere doesn't suit me. It's European style of building, there's no yard. They're just self-contained houses, and I'm used to communal living. When you come into this yard now, you see people coming and going, but out there its just empty land. Unless its compulsory, it's not the kind of place for people used to communal life . . . No. Maybe there are flowers out there, maybe the houses are painted, but you can't live on that. Slum clearance will make me lose my workshop, my customers, and my home.'[Y]

Owners and tenants alike, therefore, looked on slum clearance with alarm, and though the tenants stood to gain in value for their rent, they discounted the amenities of the estate. But was this, in part, conservatism? They had never experienced the conveniences of a modern house: would they come to appreciate them once they were moved, and value them at the price? The *Daily Times*, in periodic supplements on the progress of town planning in Lagos, reviewed enthusiastically the success of Suru Lere. Under the heading, 'Life is Superb at Suru Lere', an article in December 1958 reported, 'A name which was once the object of ridicule by dwellers of Lagos slums now inspires hope and confidence in the very people who almost did their worst to stop the Lagos Slum Clearance Scheme.'[1] 'Now they call it . . . HAPPY SURULERE!' exclaimed another *Daily Times* reporter two years later. 'Four years ago packed meetings were held in the Lagos slums to protest against the plans to clear the slums and rehouse the people . . . What is the position today? There are no protests—except from people who cannot get houses on the estate. A Lagos Executive Development Board official told me: "The thing has switched right round. People are crying out for the new houses and we are having difficulty coping with the demand." ' There were, he found, complaints about transport and trade, but the tenants he met spoke with all the fervour of converts of their new homes, to which they had so reluctantly been moved. 'If there were heavens on earth, my estate house would be one of them,' a butcher told him. 'Frankly, I felt he was overdoing it,' the reporter felt bound to admit—'especially as he added that he had difficulty in selling his meat!'[2]

But, allowing for some exaggeration, did this mean that the residents of central Lagos need not, after all, have been so much afraid?

[1] 20th December, 1958.
[2] 11th May, 1960.

8

THE REHOUSING ESTATE

FOUR miles from the centre of Lagos, by a bus terminus and suburban station, a road turns off the main north-bound highway into the village of Suru Lere. Where it crosses the railway lines, for fifty yards, stall-holders have gathered along the curb, attracting the travellers as they walk home from the bus stop. Beyond is the centre of the neighbour-hood: stained concrete façades back onto cluttered yards, and unmade side streets peter out by bungalows let out in lodgings. Further on, the road runs humped and pot-holed between rows of mud and breeze-block cottages, some half finished, the doors and windows at uncertain angles, and ends under the shady trees of a country village. South of this road, and west of the highway out of the city, is 'New Lagos'—the estates developed by the L.E.D.B. Colour-washed in ochre, pink and green, the houses march out in their contemporary uniformity against the bush. There are four kinds of development: freehold plots, for which the Board provides service roads; freehold houses; a worker's estate; and the rehousing estate. The first two are designed for the new professional class of the capital—the freehold houses, of two to six rooms, costing between £1,200 and £3,000. The worker's estate is reserved, in principle, for tenants earning less than £300 a year, and rents are subsidized. It is very similar to the rehousing estate, except that the streets are laid out less stiffly straight. Across one end of these estates runs a new highway, Western Avenue, linking the deep water port of Apapa directly with the northbound route, and nearby are the site of the Mainland Hospital and the new National Stadium.

The rehousing estate is a mile from the bus terminus at the main road. Western Avenue cuts through it, dividing it into two halves each a quarter of a mile square. In 1959 there were 913 houses, two schools, a few shops, and a small public hall. A

Back yard, central Lagos

—and in the rehousing estate

Shops, central Lagos

—and on the rehousing estate

site between the rehousing estate and the workers' estate had been set aside for a church, a clinic, and community centre. The houses are built for the most part in blocks of four, the roofs of corrugated sheeting and the walls of cement blocks, painted with bright pastel washes. Encouraged by garden competitions, some of the tenants have planted blossoming shrubs and tufts of lemon grass below their porches, and tendrils of mesembryanthemum spread their purple flowers over the red earth, softening the rectangular pattern of the streets.

The front doors open into a living room: in ninety-six houses there is no other room, and communal lavatories are provided in a separate block. In the others, the living room gives access to one or more bedrooms: 576 houses had one bedroom only—a 'room and parlour' as it would be called in Lagos—160 had two and eighty-one three bedrooms. On one side of the back door is a kitchen with built-in oven, and on the other a lavatory and shower. Behind the house is an open space which the occupants may fence and cultivate as they wish.

Everything about the estate contrasts with central Lagos. The streets are wide and empty, the doors shut, the window slats pulled down. Here and there, a woman has set a tray of cigarettes and provisions on her porch, but there is no bustle of traffic, no one passes by: only once in a while a schoolgirl may pause to buy a pennyworth of toffee. The residents leave early and return late, and their neat homes wear an air of quiet self-containment. It was this peace and isolation, the self-sufficiency of a well appointed house, which most appealed to those who liked it there: and underlay the frustration of those who hated it.

Some of the young married couples found on the estate a new independence. They enjoyed the quiet in which to study, the chance of a private life out of reach of interfering neighbours or relatives, a home of their own. They decorated their sitting rooms with fresh cotton prints and vases of artificial flowers, and had for the first time space to spread their books. They fenced their gardens and planted paw-paws and red peppers, oranges, mangoes and climbing beans. Here, in the privacy of a suburban garden, they were their own masters. 'I like it very much,' said a young clerk. 'Everyone has his own apartment—there are no worries or troubles like in Lagos. Everyone minds his own business. And I prefer living alone than with a family. Here I

H

can read a book or a novel, or listen to the radio, no-one to bother me. People make too much noise in Lagos. And living with family you must quarrel, there must be trouble. When I stay with family I don't have the chance to do as I like. Maybe the time I want to read, they will tell me to do something, or go somewhere, and as I'm their junior, I must do it.' His wife added, 'I like it for three reasons. Here I don't have to go to the public pump, that's one. And I can plant vegetables in my own plot. And here I have my own apartment. In Lagos when I was washing clothes, the landlady used to say she was washing her clothes, and no chance to spread our own.' Wives appreciated the privacy also for their children's sake. 'You know where you have family together there are quarrels and jealousies,' said a saleswoman in a department store. 'Now that I go to work, I know that no one will trouble my children while I'm away. But there, someone will flog your child before you return—even some of the tenants.'

The householders at Suru Lere who were glad to have escaped from their family group gave three reasons. Firstly, they were now free from the control of their elders. A young man who had had a restless career as a lorry driver, in the army, and then in the North, before coming to work for the Post Office in Lagos, said: 'My father was the owner of a very large compound where I was living in Lagos, but he refused to come here. So I came on my own because I didn't want to go on living any longer with my family. All my brothers and sisters are in Lagos. Actually, I find this place is better for me. When I am with my family I can't do what I like. For instance, I wanted to marry a girl, and they would not allow it. Well, I was in love with her, and she has two issues (that is, children) for me. Or I'd come back at midnight and find the door locked—too many things like that. Here they can't lock me out, I'm free to do what I like.' A well-to-do trader, who had refused herself to move to Suru Lere, made the same point about her children. 'They seem to like the life at Suru Lere. They're free from my discipline there—they can go where they like and return when they like, keep any friend they like. They're free in all sorts of ways which I kept a strict check on when they lived with me. But for that, they wouldn't prefer Suru Lere—it has many things against it compared with the life in our old home, before it was pulled down.'

Secondly, they were free from family quarrels, especially between their wives and their mothers, in which their own loyalties were divided. A young Yoruba explained: 'To live with my family brings disrespect to elders, when you see them all the time. But if you see them once in a blue moon, so to speak, there is more respect. If my mother and my wife live together now, my wife may be disrespecting my mother, and that will not be good. Even if I agree with my wife, I cannot show it to my mother. I believe in living with my wife and children separately.'

Lastly, they were free from continual demands for money. 'They don't stop to think what you can afford, anything they want, they just come to you,' a Customs clerk complained. 'Here they can't just come and demand money from me, because of the fares. It's tenpence to this place: suppose they want a shilling, they can't give tenpence fare to demand a shilling. But there, they could trek to that place any time, and if they demanded five shillings, it might be the last money I had.' Another said, 'I prefer staying alone than with my family, and seeing them occasionally, otherwise it will cost me more. Because if I live separately then I only give them what I can afford.'

Besides the independent young couples, the rehousing estate appealed particularly to outsiders who had felt at a disadvantage in the predominantly Yoruba culture of central Lagos. A prosperous contractor from Calabar explained:

What I can say I like about Suru Lere is this—it's self-contained. You know Lagos, you have other people on top of you, and perhaps they are not from your country, you can't always hear what they say—and because you do not hear each other well, there will be quarrels. But here I am just on my own, self-contained, and I don't have anything to do with my neighbour.

I have my own kitchen: what my wife cooks, no one else will know. When you have a lot of women in the same kitchen, they criticise each other all the time—'you cook what is fit for a cow', or 'you eat too much', or 'you eat too much fine food'. Again, fighting over the pump. You know these Yoruba people don't keep good discipline, especially the illiterate ones. Perhaps your child will cross over to the other side of the courtyard and quarrel with one of their children. The parents will just come out and start beating the child, without asking who is right and who is wrong. The Yoruba don't like staying with other tribes, they call them kobokobo—

and Ibos, too, they're not in co-operation with people from other places.

That's number one, and number two, a Christian can't live with a Muslim, they will be quarrelling all the time. A Muslim starts to shout at five o'clock, at the hour of prayer, when you may just be trying to get some rest—a Christian can't tolerate it. That's why every stranger likes to come up here.

The estate tended to attract, for these reasons, those who were least characteristic of the streets from which they had been moved. Ibos, and others from the Eastern Region, or outside Nigeria altogether, accounted for 31% of the sample interviewed on the rehousing estate; in central Lagos they were only 6%. There were more Christians,[1] more young men and more wage earners—particularly more clerks, who amounted to 30% of the men. The estate seemed to be selecting from the residents of central Lagos a different balance of population: from a predominantly Muslim, Yoruba, middle-aged community of traders and independent craftsmen, it attracted above all the employees of Government and commercial firms, men from the Eastern Region whose close family ties in Lagos were few, the young rebel escaping from a domineering family.

In each of these groups, the proportion who preferred their new surroundings to central Lagos was higher than for the rest. Only a quarter of the Ibo householders, for instance, regretted the move, but three-quarters of the Yoruba. As a whole, 32% of the heads of households said that they were, on balance, glad to have exchanged their old homes for the rehousing estate. A further 11% were undecided or indifferent. But 57% wished they were back in central Lagos. It seems that this last percentage might have been higher, but for those who refused even to try the experience of Suru Lere, and went elsewhere.

About a third of the residents of central Lagos had avoided the rehousing estate when their old homes were pulled down. They went to stay with relatives, evicted tenants from other property they owned, or preferred to rent cheaper accommodation at Mushin or Shomolu on the outskirts of the town. Others

[1] On the rehousing estate 71% of the men interviewed were under 40, in central Lagos 41%: 46% of all householders were wage earning compared with 37% in central Lagos: and 73% compared with 32% were Christians. There were more Christians not only because there were more Easterners: more of the Yoruba were Christians also.

had found the estate beyond their means, and left or were evicted when they could not pay the rent.

A young clerk who had been moved from a large family house said: 'When we were about to come here, most of our people didn't want to come to this bush—they call this place bush—they think there are bad spirits here. So the proportion of us who came here, in short, was only two of us out of twenty. The rest went to rent places in E.B. or Idi Oro. They think these houses here are not the kind of houses in which we Africans live—you know we live in groups, not one here, one there. And not only our own house, but most of them—I don't think you will have seen houses like this in Lagos. So I have only one relative here. She is a woman selling cloth, and since she came here, the trade has flopped. This woman is too fat, she can't be going to Lagos every time on the bus, so she had to give up. She is being assisted by her husband, who is a contractor in Lagos. She is even thinking of quitting because of the rent. They have a family house in E.B., and they have just quitted the tenant, who has been there a long time. They sued in court, and it took them two years before they quitted the man. Now she has to leave this place and go to live there. She has a brother too: that one did not come here. He could not afford the rentage in E.B., not to think of Lagos, and has to go to Agege. He is a pensioner, and if you see his condition now you will pity him.'

Many, therefore, who would suffer hardship on the estate had avoided it in the first place, or had left, and in comparing the householders in Suru Lere with central Lagos, this must be taken into account. So, although only 3% of those interviewed in central Lagos wanted to move to the rehousing estate, while a third of the residents actually on the estate preferred it to their old homes, it does not follow that the enthusiastic conversions reported by the *Daily Times* were common. However, some certainly appreciated the amenities of a modern house more than they had expected, in spite of its drawbacks. 'Before we packed over here I was looking for a place in Lagos, I didn't want to come here,' said a young man who had been living before with one of his mother's relatives in their family house. 'But now I prefer it here. It's quiet if a person wants to study.' Even so, he would have liked ideally to combine the peace of a suburb with the accessibility of the city centre. 'Though this place is airy and convenient, the main trouble is rentage, bus fares, and living allowance—I mean the cost of living. If I could have a house like this in central Lagos, I would go willingly.' Nearly everyone complained of the cost and discomfort of the journey to work, the high prices in the local shops, the dark and empty streets at night, and the qualified approval of those who preferred Suru Lere must be set against the uncompromising protest of many who wished they were back in their old homes. The majority of the householders had come to the estate reluctantly, finding no alternative, and felt that their fears had been confirmed.

THE COST OF SUBURBAN LIVING

In the first place, the cost of living on the estate was higher. Although the rents are heavily subsidised, the tenants were still paying more than they had before, partly because in central Lagos, where tenancies are of long standing, rents are exceptionally low; and partly because households occupied more space on the estate than they had before. So, although in central Lagos the average rent per room of the tenants interviewed was 38s. a month, and at Suru Lere only 25s., the average total rent on the estate was 50s.—ten shillings more than in central Lagos—since most estate tenants occupied more than one room. Rent amounted to 14% of the incomes of men in lodgings in central Lagos, 18% on the estate. Electricity—where it had not been disconnected to save money—added about 10s. to the monthly bill. Moreover, 37% of the householders at Suru Lere had been moved from houses owned by themselves or their relatives, and were mostly paying rent for the first time in their lives. Resentment against the rent was sharpened by an apparent injustice: the tenants on the workers' estate paid less for similar accommodation. 'I feel it is a sort of cheating if the people over there pay a lesser amount than we do—although we are the ones who have been deprived of their rights in Lagos,' one man said, and an old lady exclaimed indignantly, 'Would you believe it! That two-storey house there, two rooms up and one room down for two pounds ten, with kitchen and washplace. The workers on their housing estate have regular wages, but we poor people have no money. What have we done? I am a widow with no one to help me. Is it some kind of punishment on us?' An economic rent on the rehousing

estate would have been 48*s.*, on the workers' estate 50*s.*: the
rents charged were 25*s.* and 16*s.* 6*d.*, so the workers did indeed
enjoy an even more substantial subsidy. And though the workers
were restricted to those with incomes under £300 a year, only five
of the residents interviewed on the rehousing were any better off.

The cost of transport worried them even more than the rent.
It was the most universal complaint—fares to work, to get their
children to school, their wives to market. It also raised their
expenses indirectly: the men had to buy a midday meal at work,
since they could not afford to come home, and prices in the local
shops were higher because of transport charges. As one man put
it, 'Here transport is an unavoidable disease—if you want to go
any place you have to pay money. Whereas in Lagos you can
go as you like, everything is within one's reach, and food is
reasonable. This distance makes life hard here. Whatsoever foodstuffs you buy, you have to pay transport. The price in these
shops here is about 75% above cost—if you buy a bottle of beer
at the bus stop it's 2*s.* 4*d.*, here at the hotel it's 3*s.* And transport
in the morning is a headache. When the bus started in 1957 it
stopped at the police station, and only one bus. We had to cry,
cry, keep on begging till we got the second bus. Even now, if
you wait for bus here in the morning, you will never get to work
on time.' Men who travelled regularly to work by bus or train
were spending an average £2 a month on fares for their household, and the cost amounted to 15% of their incomes. Some of
the men who worked late into the night, and had to depend on
taxis, spent over £5 a month on fares. 'Transport costs us a lot,'
said a sales representative earning £24 a month. 'Myself alone
about five pounds, my wife three pounds. It's sevenpence to
Lagos by bus, but if I want to go in a hurry, two shillings for a
taxi to Yaba. And two shillings taxi every night, because I do
my work mostly in the evenings—house to house canvassing,
I work till ten or eleven at times. Then there's the children, I
give them threepence for chop money, and twopence for their
fares. That's tenpence a day for the two of them. I used to be a
heavy smoker, twenty or thirty sticks a day, I've had to give it
up entirely since we came here. And we don't buy dresses now—
all our clothes are four or five years old. I'm down to four pairs
of trousers now, and a new pair costs five or six pounds—I've
had no money for four months. I don't save anything, I spend the

whole lot. And my wife just present me with this prescription
for drugs which the doctor says will cost five pounds. Where
am I to get the money from?' Some men, to save money, walked
the six miles to work: the more fortunate bought bicycles on
loans from their employers. All had had to make economies to
make ends meet.

The householders spent about as much on food as in central
Lagos: the average for each member of the household, at 36s. a
month, is only a shilling less, and housekeeping represented only
a slightly higher proportion of the men's income. But since food
was more expensive, they ate less well. Rent, fares and food were
expenses they could not avoid, and they were forced to save in
other ways. Most seriously, they could no longer be so generous
in help to their relatives. In central Lagos, over half the heads of
households had made monthly allotments of a pound or more to
kinsfolk outside the household, and a quarter paid out over £4.
At Suru Lere, half could give nothing at all, a third gave upwards
of a pound, and only 7% over £4. A woman trader said, 'I
used to be responsible for two of my half brothers—one is my
mother's cousin's son, but I can call him my brother, the other
is my father's son—they were only young children. I used to
help with their schooling before, but when I left Lagos, I had to
refuse.' A craftsman who used to pay his mother a regular allowance remarked sadly, 'I can't do it now—and it is my duty.' And
because they could no longer afford presents, the householders
were sometimes shy of visiting relatives whom they used to help.
One young woman, for instance, had an especially affectionate
relationship with a young half sister, who was still at school.
'She treats me like a father, she asks me for anything she wants—
school books, money, clothes. I don't go to see her now—she's
sure to ask me for something, and I can't afford it. Once in a
month or two months perhaps I go, when I can scrape together
five or ten shillings.' Similarly some from the Eastern Region
could no longer afford to visit their friends at home, not only
because of the fare, but because they had nothing to take with
them. A young widow, who was almost destitute on the estate,
might have returned home for good, but for this. 'My mother
keeps worrying me to come home, she hears I am suffering too
much here. But I can't afford it, and it would be shameful to go
home without a penny after so many years.'

Their families apart, the residents also tended to give up entertainment and their membership of benefit societies, church groups and social clubs, because they could no longer afford either the fare or the subscription. 'I was a member of four clubs when I was in Lagos,' one young man remarked, a clerk who was earning a better income than most, 'a table tennis club, the Taiwo area boys' club, my father's side area boys' club, and the Campos boy's club too. I used to attend the functions regularly, almost every night. I've never been again since I came here. Even table tennis—I don't think I could hold a bat now. And cinema—I used to go to the cinema every night with my wife. But even if I could get transport, I don't think we have enough allowance for the pictures again. We used to attend dances in Lagos too, but we don't do it now. And I went to church every Sunday in Lagos too, every day in the Lenten season. Since we've been here, I don't think I've been to church more than twice.'

In spite of the economies, many of the families had got into debt since they arrived, especially in arrears of rent, and were haunted by the fear of eviction—'those lorries coming in the middle of the night! There is a great fear of them coming and turning you out, at four o'clock in the morning, and putting all your loads in the street. You can't sleep, thinking perhaps they are coming to quit you.' An L.E.D.B. memorandum of early 1959 lists ninety-eight cases where eviction for arrears had either been carried out or was under consideration—about 11% of the tenancies held at that time. Between April 1959 and the end of March 1960, 196 families were evicted. At least a fifth of the householders interviewed owed money, mostly for rent.[1]

THE EFFECT ON TRADE

The higher cost of living at Suru Lere was much more difficult to meet, because so many of the households earned less as well. Traders and independent craftsmen lost most of their business when they moved. Few if any of their former customers were willing to lose time and money on a long bus ride, when they could take their orders more conveniently elsewhere. The population of the estate itself is too small and too dispersed to support many traders or craftsmen, especially as most people go into

[1] I did not collect this information systematically, but of those asked, 36% were in debt—19% of the whole sample.

central Lagos every day and continue to buy there, where the choice is wider and prices lower. The estate lies off the main roads, and attracts few outsiders. Moreover, the people of the older Suru Lere village have pre-empted the best sites for market stalls along the road to the city centre. Even those on the estate who still worked from a shop or stall in central Lagos found that business suffered. They were no longer accessible to customers at home; lost time in travelling and could not supervise their apprentices so thoroughly; and since they could not carry their stock home every night, had new expenses in storage or guards.

Most of the people interviewed on the estate who had been traders or independent craftsmen were therefore in real difficulties: some destitute. A shoemaker I went to interview greeted me with the comment, 'I am alone working. Alone playing, I should say. When I was in Lagos I would reluctantly give you half an hour. Now, if you want five hours . . .' He explained, 'Before I moved here, I was first class shoemaker having shoe-making machine. I had a shop—that was Broad Street—and if you see the condition of my shop in Lagos you will like to repair your shoes there. It was my father's occupation, so I have sufficient tools. When I was there, I had a certain contract with the police force, and another from the Elder Dempster Co. for the crew's shoes. And the crews themselves when they come from England, they bring their shoes for repair. Broad Street is not far from the Customs. Murray Street (where he lived) is even nearer, only one street cross us. All now—nothing from there now.' He used to make £200 or £300 a year. 'Since I came here, not sufficient money to rent a shop here, let alone work there. This is what I have since Monday—it is 4s. 6d., and when I took it to the owner he said, "Didn't you know? This is not like Lagos, I will come for it when I have got money." From Monday now, I've got one threepence, this morning. If you look at the street now, you will not see a single man. They have all gone to Lagos, and take their shoes there for repair . . . This is not a place, but a punishment from God.' A butcher who had made 20s. to 30s. a day in Lagos, selling from a market stall, had used up all his capital on fares and meeting the higher cost of living, and his trade declined until he was virtually destitute. 'Everything has changed against me. I've never had anything like this happen to me since I was born. It seems like being taken from happiness to misery.' A dressmaker had been almost as unfortunate. 'I printed cards and gave them out,' she said, 'but they say they can't come the long journey, there are so many tailors in Lagos. All these people here, they go to Lagos to buy, give all their business to traders in Lagos. They only come here to sleep. There's nothing at all here. They say we should take one of the shops here—but there's no one to patronise. I cut out paper patterns for the girls here sometimes, and that's all, except baby dresses occasionally—two or three shillings. Business is paralysed.'

Two of the craftsmen had given up working on their own account since they moved to the estate. 'If they didn't see me at the shop, they used to come to my house—they always found me if they wanted me. Before I moved here I was always getting sufficient money,' said a carpenter. 'When I come here I lose my customers, and no one knows me, so the money I am getting is only two pounds, one pound, a few shillings, tobacco . . . I had to give up.' He had found a job in the Public Works Department, where his income was steadier, but averaged several pounds less than when he was his own master. Most of the men still self-employed made less: as a whole, their profits had fallen by an average of £8 a month since they moved to the estate. Only a carver selling to Europeans; a moneylender who, by special arrangement, had come from outside the slum clearance area; and a trader who sent his goods to Kano for sale were unaffected. Many traders and independent craftsmen must have avoided the estate in the first place, since over half the men interviewed in central Lagos were self employed, but only a quarter at Suru Lere.

As most of the men on the estate worked for a wage, their personal earnings had not been directly affected. The average income of all the men was £15 10s. a month, 12s. more than amongst the wage earners in central Lagos, where there were relatively fewer clerks. But this figure is over £8 below the average of all men interviewed in central Lagos, so the estate was a relatively less prosperous neighbourhood: the successful independent men preferred to go elsewhere.

The women suffered more. Most of them had been traders or dressmakers in Lagos, and the incomes of the women interviewed had fallen by an average of £10 since they came to the estate. Only four of the twenty-two were no worse off—a clerk, a woman with a stall in central Lagos, where she spent all her time, and two who had already retired from work. Altogether, they earned an average of £2 19*s*. o*d*. a month: the women interviewed in central Lagos had almost four times as much, partly because many more were working. The wives of the householders interviewed were equally affected. A quarter had given up any attempt to trade, while as many had lost most of their business but still struggled, rather hopelessly, to scrape together a few shillings in the month. They were hampered because petty trading was not strictly allowed, and they hesitated to set out their wares until the local government officers had gone home for the day: often the food sellers gave away the rice they had prepared to children, since they could not sell it. Only 60% of the wives on the rehousing estate were earning and almost a quarter of these were employed in shops and offices, compared with 95% of the wives in central Lagos, nearly all traders or dress-makers. Altogether, the estate wives made only 45*s*. a month on average, as against nearly £9 for the wives in central Lagos. They had to depend more on their husbands, and some men did in fact give more substantial allowances to their wives, mostly at the expense of other family obligations.

The rehousing estate had, therefore, all the disadvantages to a trader that its isolation and dispersed population would suggest. Central Lagos is the hub of the city, alive from early morning until late at night: 'It is Canaan to us,' said a woman trader, 'a land of milk and honey.' Suru Lere is deserted for most of the day, and its only thoroughfare skirts rather than crosses the estate. So there were fewer traders at Suru Lere, and more women not working at all, and those who still traded made much less by it. In central Lagos the average profit of all the traders in the households interviewed was £11 12*s*. 4*d*.; on the rehousing estate it was £4 1*s*. 9*d*. One old lady was driven to exclaim: 'May God deliver me out of this place.'

THE EFFECT ON FAMILY RELATIONSHIPS

As they had feared, the households not only paid out more to live on the estate, but also—taking the wives' earnings with the husband's—mostly had less to spend. They could not therefore

give their relatives as much help as before they were moved.
Nor could they visit them as often, since they now lived much
further away. Slum clearance had scattered the family group,
and to be out of reach of their kinsfolk distressed the majority as
much as it pleased a few. The fresh air of Suru Lere might be
healthy, but their family life contracted in such chill seclusion.

A comparison of the two samples of households shows that
the residents on the estate were relatively isolated. The proportion of parents, and brothers and sisters, living within a mile is
more than halved, and their isolation from any members of their
husband's or wives' families is even more complete. These
differences are not, of course, necessarily the result of slum
clearance. As we have already seen, the two samples already
differed in age structure and ethnic origin. But, in so far as their
influence can be determined with the small numbers available,
these other differences do not seem to account for the attenuation
of kinship ties on the estate.[1]

TABLE VII: HOUSEHOLDERS WITH RELATIVES WITHIN
A MILE CENTRAL LAGOS AND SURU LERE

Percentage of household heads* with:	*Central Lagos* (100%=)		*Rehousing Estate* (100%=)	
mother within a mile	44%	(63)	15%	(32)
father within a mile	17%	(29)	8%	(12)
a brother within a mile	54%	(81)	27%	(41)
a sister within a mile	37%	(71)	15%	(39)
a half brother or sister	59%	(75)	35%	(46)
husband/wife's mother	38%	(68)	15%	(33)
husband/wife's father	25%	(49)	14%	(21)
husband/wife's brother or sister	60%	(90)	13%	(46)

* Excluding those who had no mother etc. living.

In all, 39% of the brothers and sisters of the central Lagos
sample had lived within a mile, and 60% of their children over

[1] There were more Easterners on the rehousing estate, who might be expected to
have fewer of their relatives in Lagos. But the differences between the two samples
do not arise from this—they are almost as great when Easterners are excluded.
For instance, taking only the brothers and sisters of those born in Lagos or the
Western Region, the percentage within a mile drops from 40% to 20%—of children
over sixteen, from 83% to 68%.

16. At Suru Lere, the percentages were 15 and 47. Fewer, too, were living with relatives. In central Lagos, 16% whose mother was still alive shared the same house with her: at Suru Lere only 6%. The proportions sharing a house with one of their brothers or sisters, or with their half brothers or sisters, were halved on the estate; while those with six or more adult relatives in the same house fell from 23% to 5%. Since the houses at Suru Lere are smaller, in some cases the relatives might still be close by, the family from one large dwelling divided into several houses. Though they could then remain together, they still had to find the money to pay for several tenancies.

The radius of a mile encompasses, in central Lagos, the densely built western end of Lagos Island, but at Suru Lere, only the relatively thinly populated area from the estate to the bus terminus on the main road. So, except for the relatives who lived with them, or had also been rehoused on the estate, the residents at Suru Lere had to travel back into town to see their family—a long walk to the bus stop, and then a tedious journey of an hour or more. So they paid fewer visits: leaving early and returning late, they made as many calls as they could on their way to and from work. Once home, they were usually too tired to go out again, even if they could afford it. And they received fewer visitors. As they explained, their relatives found Suru Lere too isolated: fares were too expensive, they lacked time for the journey, got tired of waiting for the bus, or were even unable to find the address when they arrived.

> We used to see them almost every day when we were in Lagos, sometimes two or three times. But they don't come because of the transport, and they think this place is far.

> The slum clearance has scattered us. Apart from those of the same father and mother, I don't see my family again. All other family is scattered, some at Shomolu, some Agege, some of them have gone to the bush to their villages. I've not been able to see some of my family for two years, and I don't even know where they are.

> I don't see my sister at all unless I force myself there. If you don't go to see them they don't come. Sometimes I visit them four times before they come—they don't like this side. They have to change bus six times.

> When I was in Lagos they were with me. We live in the same

The Rehousing Estate

street. Old wife's family, new wife's family, we see each other every day. In Lagos you see everybody nearly every day. Do you see any of my family visiting me here?

On Saturday I made 5s. gain, and I ran to see my mother. I've not seen her since Saturday, and God knows when I shall see her again. She wept when I was to leave, because she didn't want to leave me, and she is afraid to come here. When I was in Lagos there was not a day I don't see her.

So the residents at Suru Lere could not maintain such close contact with their relatives. They saw fewer every week than the householders in central Lagos, and correspondingly more of them infrequently.

TABLE VIII

HOUSEHOLDERS CONTACTS WITH RELATIVES
CENTRAL LAGOS AND SURU LERE

Percentage of household heads* who saw	weekly		not within a month**	
	Central Lagos	rehousing estate	Central Lagos	rehousing estate
mother	67%	46%	14%	27%
father	38%	58%	24%	34%
a brother	65%	58%	15%	37%
a sister	57%	38%	25%	36%
a half-brother or sister	73%	61%	15%	24%
husband/wife's mother	59%	33%	22%	37%
husband/wife's father	49%	23%	29%	48%
husband/wife's brother or sister	61%	35%	21%	43%

* excluding those who had no mother etc. living. The numbers equal to 100% are as in the preceding table.
** that is, average frequency of meeting. Not within a month means that no brother, sister etc. was seen as often as once a month on average. Altogether, 24% of brothers and sisters of the central Lagos householders were seen less than monthly, 37% of those of the estate residents. The percentages seen weekly are 60% and 40% respectively.

Except for their fathers—where the numbers are too few to be very meaningful—the trend is consistent. The householders also saw 12% fewer of their adult children every week: but, more

III

strikingly, while all the householders in central Lagos with grown sons or daughters had seen at least one within a month, at Suru Lere 10% had seen none of their sons, and 32% none of their daughters within a month.[1]

This attenuation of family relationships is even more noticeable in the day to day visits exchanged between close relatives. Though the proportion of mothers and brothers and sisters seen weekly dropped by a third at Suru Lere, the proportion seen daily dropped by half.

The more formal cohesion of the family also suffered: 61% of those interviewed in central Lagos were members of a regular family meeting, but only 27% at Suru Lere—either because they no longer attended, or because the meetings had been abandoned with the demolition of the family property. Even where the meeting was still held, fewer came. 'All these meetings I told you of were when we were in Lagos: when the slum came, it scattered us,' one man remarked. He was the most senior of his family, and the meeting was still held at his home on the estate. But it was now fortnightly instead of weekly, and attendance had dropped from thirty to five. 'When we came here, you only got those of the same father. Last Saturday we had a meeting, there were only five. But before there would be my aunt, her children, my brother's children . . . This place is far, number one. Money to come, number two.'

Slum clearance, therefore, meant that family groups tended to be disrupted. This could be especially hard for old people, who had lived in family property, and been cared for by relatives around them. Their relatives elsewhere were no longer so aware of their needs, and they themselves could not afford the fare to go and ask for their help. And they were likely to be in more need of help, since they now had rent to pay, when before they had often themselves been landlords, or been able to trade. 'There's plenty of breeze and it's quiet here,' said an old woman, who had been moved from her uncle's house. 'But this seems to be a sort of hidden place—some of my family have never been able to find me here. And if you think of going to see them, you have to think of transport . . . there's a proverb says there's no good in a fine house where there's no happiness. Its by the grace

[1] As a whole, the proportion of children seen less than monthly rose from 5% in central Lagos to 22% in the rehousing estate.

Housing in the slum clearance area

Street scene in central Lagos

—and in the rehousing estate

of God that you find me still alive. I've tasted nothing since morning, and I'm not fasting yet. The money I'd have spent on food has all gone on light. I handed over six and threepence this morning.'ᵞ The plight of old people worried the young men of the estate, who felt responsible for them, very much. 'Some of our people—old people like our fathers—some of them don't have any work, and they have never been used to paying rent before. Landlords become debtors here, and the L.E.D.B. drives them away without trying to get them some little job. It causes the premature death of old people. They are forced to the villages, and they are not used to village life. They lose some of their family, where they were living free before. There were thirty died in one year. You know, as we pass out of school we are catering for the family—our fathers may not be able to work again. But this family separation, there is no one to care for them as before. Some people are not seeing their family even for a year, who used to see them daily before—not for twelve months, twelve calendar months!'

Their families apart, other social relationships also suffered. Fewer than in central Lagos were members of religious groups, friendly or welfare societies, social clubs, and they could see less of their friends. Even on the estate itself, the privacy of each home tended to isolate neighbours from each other: though the communal life of a compound sometimes breaks down in quarrels, in central Lagos there was always someone to help in trouble. But at Suru Lere it might pass unnoticed. As one husband remarked, 'For instance now, my wife fell sick while I was away at work this morning, and no one knew about it until I got home. There was no one at home with her. If we had been in our old home now, someone would have given her first aid already.'

The isolation of the estate, therefore, impoverished social life and disrupted the family. And though some couple were compensated by the gardens and peace, sanitation and piped water, a new-found freedom from interfering relatives and quarrelsome neighbours, these were luxuries most residents could not afford. They were not self-sufficient, and could not exploit their independence to make more of their domestic life. So far from husband and wife drawing together in a more intimate relationship, they were sometimes forced to separate. Unable to meet the expenses of suburban life, some of the husbands sent their wives home to their families, and distributed their children amongst relatives who could care for them. Wives, finding no opportunity for trade, left to live with their own relatives nearer the centre of the city: others simply deserted when their husbands could no longer support them. One man, who had been particularly unluck, said of his junior wife, 'I hadn't a penny to put down for her, so she had to desert me, she said she couldn't stay here to starve.' Another had sent his wife to her mother on Lagos Island. 'I can't keep her here when I can't maintain her.' He went to see her once a month. 'It's no use going when you can only put your hand in an empty pocket.' A van driver said, 'When I was in Lagos, I never pay for house, I had money. I could have financed my wife with something to sell. Now the house is pulled down it change everything. She is every time crying, fighting, worrying me for money. Even yesterday I told her to quit if she kept on worrying me for money: I can't steal.' 27% of the married men had been divorced at some time, 9% more than in the central Lagos sample, and at least in some cases the quarrels had arisen out of the difficulties they experienced since they were moved.

Even when there had been no quarrel, husbands and wives spent more time apart. In central Lagos 81% of the married heads of households had seen husband or wife within a day: at Suru Lere only 64%. The more scattered the family group, the more difficult it is to fulfil obligations without absence from home. The poorer people are, the greater the strain on the loyalty of husband or wife, and the competing claims of marriage and kin are less easily reconciled.

Slum clearance, therefore, meant much more than exchange of a shoddy home in a convenient neighbourhood for a convenient home at the end of a tiresome journey. The combination of isolation, higher expenses and lower incomes threatened the basis of their way of life. They not only saw less of their relatives, but the quality of the relationships changed. In central Lagos, even though the communal family houses were gradually being broken up, the unity of the extended family survived in day to day visits, in regular meetings and mutual help. But the families on the estate were finding it less and less easy to maintain these visits or discharge their obligations. They were forced into a self-sufficiency alien to their traditions, and harassed by the demands on their over-stretched resources, some households began to break up. These hardships are summed up in the experience of a motor mechanic, an independent craftsman who had been a tenant in central Lagos for seven years before his home was pulled down. Slum clearance had halved his income, ruined his wife and sister's trade, forced him to sell his bicycle, his furniture, and dismiss his wife's servant, obliged him not to visit his relatives so often, and halved the support he could give his own and his wife's mother, apart from the many other members of his family who used to appeal to him, and whom he could no longer help. Now it threatened to leave him homeless. He was eighteen pounds in arrears of rent, and threatened with immediate notice to quit. He had even thought seriously of going abroad, out of reach of all his family responsibilities, in a last effort to recover his fortunes. For many like him, the amenities of a modern house had been forced on them at a sacrifice they could not afford.

In emphasising the hardships which the slum clearance scheme entailed, I do not mean to disparage its aim. But the problems are intricate and serious, as they must be when a whole community is dislodged, and it would be wrong to underestimate them. In a society where most people can barely live within their income, any disturbance creates great difficulties. For the people of central Lagos, these difficulties are especially serious, because they depend so much on trade, which is notoriously hard to transplant. There is a danger that their family life will be impoverished as much as their livelihood, and in turn create new hardships as they are forced to abandon obligations to their kin. Good housing is very much needed in Lagos, and a nation naturally desires a fine appearance for its capital city. But unless these aims can be reconciled with the needs and resources of the people who must be displaced, the harm done will be disproportionate to the achievement.

9

REHOUSING AS SOCIAL POLICY

We have at last become conscious of slum areas. That is undoubtedly some gain though, by itself, it does not take us far. The consciousness of this problem has brought the realization of its urgency and, at the same time, of its magnitude. Looking at these slums and the sub-human conditions in which men and women live there, we feel that immediate action must be taken to change all this. And then the vastness of the problem confronts us and we feel a little overwhelmed.

... Action is initiated, but progress is slow because of innumerable difficulties. Vested interests are always hard to dislodge and the law generally appears to favour them. But the real difficulty is the lack of accommodation for those who live in the slum areas at present. We have to provide housing for them before we can ask them to vacate. When we try to do this, those very people, whom we seek to benefit, raise difficulties and are reluctant to move. This is to some extent understandable, for their lives and work have revolved near that area and to take them far away means to uproot them from their work. Also, whatever new accommodation might be provided, is likely to have a higher rent, even though it might be subsidised ...

The more one has looked at this problem of the slums, the more it becomes something far bigger than the mere building of new houses. It is intimately connected with occupations and work and the general economy of that place. It has to face ingrained habits and a lack of desire as well as a lack of training to use better accommodation.

So wrote Jawaharlal Nehru, Prime Minister of India, about the slums of Old Delhi in 1958.[1] His analysis applies with almost equal cogency to the problems of slum clearance in Lagos. Even in countries with far greater resources, similar difficulties may arise: a study of housing problems in

[1] In a forward to *Slums of Old Delhi*, A Survey Report by Bharat Sevak Samaj Delhi Pradesh.

London showed how long journeys to work, lack of jobs for women in the suburbs, and particularly the disruption of family ties, gave rise to anxiety and loneliness. The kind of hardship suffered by the men and women described in this study illustrate a general problem: how are changes in the physical surroundings of people's lives to be co-ordinated with their social and economic circumstances.

A slum clearance policy is not necessarily mistaken because the people moved at first suffer by it. The disruption of their way of life may be an unavoidable consequence of reform. In spite of the razed plots where, after five years, scarcely a single new building had gone up, in spite of the harassed and frustrated households at Suru Lere, the loss of trade and scattered families, the L.E.D.B. went on with their work. They were neither ignorant of these problems, nor indifferent to them. They were carrying out a Government policy for which there was widespread support, and they believed that even at the cost of some hardship, slum clearance was right. The working out of a fair housing policy depends not only on the hardship that may result, but on how far national interests may in justice override the interests of a few.

The problems of the Lagos scheme can only be understood in the light of the reasons which distinguished central Lagos as an area of particular concern. The arguments for slum clearance in any one neighbourhood have to be set against other possible uses of capital resources. The economic programme of the Federal Government for 1955–60 proposed to spend two and a half million pounds in clearing central Lagos—more than on either the development of industry or higher education in the whole of Nigeria, and as much as on the medical services of the city.[1] At the same time, the programme provided for only a preliminary investigation of the Lagos Sewage Scheme,

---

[1] *The Economic Programme of the Government of the Federation of Nigeria,* 1955–60 (Lagos, Federal Government Printer, 1956). The total capital requirement for the Lagos slum clearance scheme was £2,670,000: for industry £1,315,000; for higher education £1,401,000; and for medical service £2,591,000. Much of the capital for slum clearance was to be provided in Federal loans to the L.E.D.B., so these figures show the immediate, not necessarily the eventual cost of the Federal Government. It is still a remarkable proportion of the capital available. In 1959, the L.E.D.B. estimated the gross cost of the scheme at almost £7 million, from which they expected a return of £4 million—a net cost of just under £3 million.

recommended by the International Bank Mission of 1954, which was estimated to cost five millions, and would, as the programme admitted, 'probably be the most important single contribution which could be made towards improving the health of the inhabitants of Lagos and thus restricting the ever-increasing cost of curative measures.'

To release funds for slum clearance, then, other measures had to be postponed which might have done more for the health of the city. The influence of living conditions on health in a tropical city has not been thoroughly studied: it may be, for instance, that where people live so much out of doors, overcrowding is less serious than in a colder climate. Nor are space and amenities the only considerations. Some of the families moved to the rehousing estate may actually have suffered in their health. They ate less well, were more tired and worried, could less easily afford medical attention, and had further to go to find it. Also, it happens that central Lagos is remarkably free of mosquitoes, while parts of the rehousing estate, near uncultivated land, were plagued with them. The walls of some houses were blackened all over with the remains of swatted insects. Several people complained that they or their children had suffered from malaria for the first time in their lives on the estate. So, although better housing is surely relevant, its priority on grounds of health alone is at least open to argument.

But, health apart, the overcrowding, inflated rents, discomfort and indignity of so much accommodation in Lagos would have justified a vigorous policy in their own right. All the same, central Lagos is probably the most intractable neighbourhood in which the problem could have been tackled. There are other parts of the city where housing is as bad, and where there is no long established family property, rents are higher, and the residents already have to make long and tiresome journeys to their work. Moreover, the worst of Lagos housing is not so much the condition of the buildings as their overcrowding. While the population grows continually, and the landlords can charge a year's exhorbitant rent in advance for the meanest accommodation, the most urgent need is not to pull houses down, but to provide more of a decent standard. As it is, thousands of the residents who have moved from central Lagos will find their own lodgings in the suburbs, as bad or worse than any they have left, and add to the congestion of the new slums fast overwhelming the outskirts of the city.[1] Though the L.E.D.B. has tried to regulate this suburban development, its measures have been mainly restrictive, and have often only had the effect of driving people across the township boundary, where control is less strict. If the money voted to slum clearance in central Lagos had been used instead to reform and develop the outlying communities of the township, it could have forestalled the growth of new slums at less cost and hardship, and would have relieved more effectively the congestion of the city. The improvement of health and housing, therefore, would not in themselves have led most logically to the concentration of effort in central Lagos.

But it was not primarily concern at unhealthy conditions and overcrowding which carried the slum clearance scheme forward so insistently. Whatever other arguments might be brought forward, the old streets were above all, in the words of the Economic Programme, 'a disgrace to the capital of Nigeria'. 'A humiliation to any person with a sense of national pride,' the Minister of Lagos affairs had said—not only for what they were in themselves, but for the scorn they must arouse in visitors from those nations which for centuries had exploited, ruled and patronised West Africa. The overriding aim was to rebuild the most conspicuous neighbourhood of Lagos to the standard Nigerians had set themselves, as a matter of pride, and a symbol of the progress they were determined to achieve. And by this token of their intentions, rather than their present wealth, they hoped the foreign visitor would judge them.

This is not to say that national pride was the only reason for slum clearance, or even its most important object: but it is the only reason which could justify the clearance of central Lagos, rather than any other neighbourhood of the city. It is also the reason why the execution of the scheme presented such intractable problems.

THE FUTURE OF CENTRAL LAGOS

For the advocates of slum clearance, as much as for those dispossessed, the most serious disappointment of the scheme was

[1] The report of the Federal Medical Services for 1958 comments, 'This problem (of overcrowding) is certainly very much with us and as the slums in the centre of Lagos Island are cleared, new ones are simultaneously created on the mainland.' p. 1.

the failure of the former owners to rebuild. The promise to reconvey their land to them had failed to win their support, but still frustrated any alternative plan for its use. Even when they held their compensation intact, the owners could not meet the additional charge of 20% and rebuild to the standard required; and often the compensation had been sub-divided; or dissipated in meeting the hardships of removal. In effect, the provisions of the scheme put onto the former owners themselves the responsibility of rebuilding central Lagos to the standard which prestige demanded.

At the time of writing, it seems that a few owners might be able to recover their freehold by leasing the property to a commercial firm. The firm would advance the cost of the land in return for a long lease, and the family then retained the freehold at the sacrifice of any income or use of it for many years.[1] Even if they could plan far enough into the future to accept this arrangement, they still had to find somewhere to live meanwhile. It meant besides that the property would be occupied by expatriate firms which alone had the capital to offer such terms, and this would be very widely resented. The scheme had been attacked at its inception on the grounds that the land would pass to aliens, and the promise to the former owners had been intended as a safeguard against it. This promise now seems ironically to be leading to the very result it had been designed to prevent.

Only if the rate of compensation were much increased, building loans at low rates of interest made available without limit, and the standards of housing relaxed, would many of the former owners be able to build. Most of them would prefer this way out of their difficulties. But it would require a generous subsidy for a development that might not achieve any radical improvement in the appearance of the capital. The owners wanted houses with many rooms, which they could build cheaply, and which would provide both a family home and a place of work for their trade or craft. But the public wanted buildings to which they could point with pride—modern shop fronts, tall blocks with well-appointed flats, pavements uncluttered by petty traders. Even

---

[1] By 1961, a few plots had in fact been leased out in this way to commercial firms, who had built four- or five-storey office blocks, rising here and there like artificial teeth in a decaying jaw. Only one of the former owners was attempting to rebuild for himself.

if the owners were more generously helped to rebuild, their needs are not really compatible with the demands of national pride.

Alternatively, if central Lagos were rebuilt on behalf of the former owners from public funds, a high standard of building could be ensured, but at even greater expense. The buildings would have to reach many storeys to rehouse the present population without overcrowding, and still leave space for roads, shops and markets. The occupiers could only afford to repay a fraction of this cost.

Either solution would strain the resources of the Federal Government. But if central Lagos is to be rebuilt without dispossessing the original owners, a further heavy capital commitment is inescapable. It would, however, be possible to make a superficial improvement without pulling down the neighbourhood at all. If new roads were put through, the lanes ditched and repaved, the houses refurbished, the most obtrusive squalor would be out of sight. There is little to be said for this on grounds of health or overcrowding, but an enclave of such gaily painted alleys in the heart of the city would at least present an appearance of great charm. And when so few African cities have preserved anything of their past, it would have a unique historical value. If this seems mere whitewashing, and the more radical reforms too costly, there is no alternative but to break the promise to restore the original owners to their land.

The freeholders of central Lagos would probably be very reluctant to release the government from their undertaking. Apart from any economic advantage, families have a deep attachment to land which has been theirs for generations, and which they feel they hold in trust for their descendants. Yet, even from the point of view of the owning families themselves, there would be some advantages in surrendering their option. The security of a new family home which they could afford, even at the cost of permanent removal from central Lagos, would be better than their present anxiety, which is beginning to disrupt families even before they are moved. Indeed, some members of the family would be better protected if they could re-establish themselves in a new permanent home as soon as they were moved. There would be less danger of compensation being dissipated, or the family split. If the owners could be compensated by a new house, rather than in cash, the risk of hardship would be even less, especially to relatives who had no personal right in the ownership of the house where they lived. Non-resident members only think of claiming their share in the property, because its value has been realized in cash. They would be most unlikely to demand the sale of a new house, and under customary law they might not be able to enforce it. So an exchange would protect the interests of the occupiers of family houses against those who stand to gain by distributing its worth.

Already, under the present scheme, there are freehold plots and houses at Suru Lere, on the estates developed by the L.E.D.B., which families moved from the slum area could have afforded out of the compensation paid to them. But the distance from the centre is too great. The displaced owners would have to be provided with sites much nearer their old homes: there is, for instance, reclaimed land within two miles of central Lagos, where sites are available and the style of building need not be pretentious. Even so, the traders displaced would still lose their most valuable asset, a central position. So in replanning the centre, shops and market stalls would have to be set aside for them at rents they could afford. These provisions should protect the former owners from serious economic hardship, and disturb their family ties as little as possible. Central Lagos could then be replanned, in the interests of the community as a whole, as a city centre of which Nigerians could be proud.

Detailed discussion of the design of such a centre lies outside the scope of a sociological study, but three main kinds of development would have to be taken into account. Firstly, to reduce the strain on public funds, either sites or buildings would have to be provided for lease as offices and luxury flats to those who could afford their economic price. Secondly, the development would hardly be viable if it ignored the market women and petty traders who animate the streets of Lagos. Sooner or later they would break down any bar, overwhelming every corner and pavement, whatever the intentions of the plan. But if footways were separated from traffic, congestion could be avoided without suppressing the spontaneity of trade, or destroying the dignity of design. Thirdly, there are tenants now in central Lagos who depend even more than owners on living near their work, for whom subsidized accommodation would have to be included in the plan of a new central area. Reconstruction on these lines would still be very expensive, but more of the initial capital would be recovered than if, as promised, the whole area were reserved for its former residents.

Apart from refurbishing the streets as they stand, it seems that any other proposal must cost far more than the present scheme. But this scheme has so far failed to achieve its aim, just because it seriously underestimated the burden the government would have to bear, if central Lagos were to be rebuilt as the nation hoped. Too much was expected of the owners to be rehoused. By compensating them at the market value of the property pulled down, but requiring them to rebuild to an altogether higher standard, the scheme left unresolved the most difficult question: where was the money to come from to provide a style of urban architecture which most Nigerians cannot yet afford? At the same time, too little was allowed for the hardship of disturbance, so that even the resources which the owners did possess were whittled away in meeting their losses. When the real cost to the nation, both in capital and subsidies, is taken into account, it becomes clear what a heavy undertaking prestige building must be, when it reaches beyond the resources of one generation to set a standard for the next. Such building may still be worthwhile, but it is neither practicable or fair to expect the families to be displaced to bear any substantial part of the cost.

THE FUTURE OF THE REHOUSING ESTATE

Whatever the fate of central Lagos, the rehousing estate will remain. The anxieties of its residents are characteristic of all new neighbourhoods brought into being by slum clearance. Wherever communities are transplanted, familiar complaints arise—of rising expenses, longer journeys, family relationships disrupted, and business lost: and the poorer they are, the less resiliently they can withstand these hardships. Town planners often act as if the buildings they provide would themselves restore those social and economic losses: if there is a community centre, there will be a community, if shops, then trade. But new social and economic relationships obstinately refuse to form about the planned facilities. In Johannesburg, Nairobi, Lagos, or London, the same contrasts set off the old communities from the new: all the genial warmth and spontaneity of life flows into the over-crowded, dilapidated streets of the long-settled neighbourhoods, and the municipal estates remain barren in their suburban propriety.

In time, these estates might grow into a life of their own, but the way they have come into being itself inhibits their growth. Unlike the old streets, they are built once for all, regulated, peopled, fixed by the plan which conceived them. However difficult it is to predetermine how people will wish to live in new surroundings, the town planner, briefed to evacuate a slum, cannot wait upon the event. If he misinterprets their needs, they may have very little freedom to develop their community in a way which suits them better.

The distance from work and relatives stands out as the crucial drawback of the new estate. Suburban life needs convenient and cheap trasnport, telephones, delivery vans, doctors who can call, a reliance on the written word and impersonal relationships—facilities to which the people are not used, and which for the most part they cannot afford. When the residents at Suru Lere tried to maintain their accustomed patterns of trade and family life, they found the six-mile journey back to the centre too slow, too tiring and too expensive. But they could not instead re-establish their social and economic life on the estate itself.

The frustration of traders and craftsmen at Suru Lere seems to have arisen above all from the difficulty of transplanting a commercial tradition which depends upon concentration. As agricultural countries develop a nationwide commerce and administration, the largest cities draw an increasing population from the countryside. The most profitable markets for goods and services develop in the centre of these cities, where petty traders and casual workers can pick up a living from the extreme con-centration of commercial life. This concentration seems to arise in part because a tradition of personal dealing has survived from an illiterate society, and in part from lack of capital. Few whole-salers or retailers have the resources to carry large stocks and run their own system of distribution. They buy and sell on short-term credits, so that goods pass rapidly through a chain of middle-men until they reach the customer in quantities he can afford. A dealer needs an intimate knowledge of current demand, and a network of informal personal contacts close at hand to make a profit in this highly competitive market. A petty trader depends upon extending credit to a group of customers she knows well, or on a pitch where crowds of people pass every day. If traders are dispersed into the suburbs, they lose their contacts, and they cannot replace them, because the dispersal of population is not matched by a corresponding dispersal of commercial life.

The loss to traders and independent craftsmen, therefore, cannot be restored by providing local shops and markets within the suburban estates. Not only are the neighbourhoods too sparse, but the scale of these markets will be too small to attract even local customers from the variety displayed at the city centre. The few market stalls provided on the rehousing estate had been abandoned, and the one street of shops never fully occupied. All the housewives complained of the lack of a market, but their own custom was not enough to sustain the kind of market which would have attracted them.

New commercial centres can only be brought to life at focal points in the suburbs, where people converge. The only suitable site at Suru Lere lay off the rehousing estate, near the bus terminus and railway station, where the road to all the estates joins the main northbound highway. Land had, in fact, been pegged out for a market here, but at the time of writing, the Town Council had not yet found the money to build it.[1] It was urgently needed, and if stalls there were reserved for traders from the rehousing estate, some of them at least would be able to re-establish a profitable business. The site could be expanded into a more comprehensive commercial centre: shopkeepers and craftsmen would have a much better prospect there than on the estate itself, if inexpensive premises were built for them. But for many of the present residents it was already too late: their capital had been irretrievably exhausted in the struggle to live.

But even a well-sited market at Suru Lere is unlikely ever to replace the unique advantages of central Lagos, and some traders will have to find another livelihood. If, as has been argued, the number of middlemen in the economy is disproportionate

[1] It was still not built at the beginning of 1961. Meanwhile the L.E.D.B. had set aside a space behind the shops on the estate, where residents might put up market stalls free of charge. The Town Council, as the controller of markets, then took over the scheme, but proposed a stall fee of five shillings a month. The residents lost interest, and the offer was not taken up.

to the productive workers, such a redistribution of incomes is to to be encouraged. But it depends on the development of industrial estates within easy reach of home, particularly if the industry is to attract women, who are the majority of traders. Factory work nearby would have appealed to many women on the estate more than trade: it would have paid them better, and offered a more secure income. As one woman said, 'We'd like a job. You go morning, come back, sleep, go morning, come back, sleep, and at the end of the month get salary. Ah thanks!'

For most women, however, the choice did not lie between trade and employment, but between trade or not working at all. Even factories and offices which did not draw on the labour of the estate would benefit the residents indirectly, since street trading would then become more profitable again. The more people brought to the neighbourhood—to work, to visit the new hospital, or the National Stadium—the more custom for snacks, soft drinks, cigarettes, the stock in trade especially of wives who lack the time or money to run a market stall.

At present, street trading is officially prohibited on the estate, as it is also in parts of Lagos. It is held to be unhygienic, to spread infection and cause congestion. But in central Lagos the press of people is such that petty trading itself cannot make much difference, while at Suru Lere there is space enough for a tray of goods on the porch, without disturbing the light traffic of the streets.

These criticisms on grounds of health seem to gather their force from a less rational prejudice against a pattern of commercial life, which is thought to be contemptible because it has been superseded in much richer economies. It seems more sensible to cancel regulations against street trading which are both unenforceable and doubtfully necessary.

If street trading were allowed, light industry encouraged and a market established, the economic life of the neighbourhood might grow in time to meet the needs of its inhabitants. At the same time, if the households moved to the estate are to re-establish their family life, it is equally important to provide for the growth of ties of kinship within the community. The ramification of family connections probably does more to integrate a neighbourhood than any other social relationships. But the terraced cottages of the rehousing estate cannot expand with the families which occupy them. The generation growing to maturity will be forced to leave home: it will even have to leave the estate altogether, unless tenancies are set aside from the needs of slum clearance. Only if, as time goes by, tenancies are allocated more and more in the interests of established residents, will the people of Suru Lere be able to draw their families around them again.

Yet the re-integration of family life will still be handicapped, because the design of the houses themselves repudiates so uncompromisingly the traditional pattern of residence. The problem is not peculiar to Lagos: town planners concerned with tropical societies have often pointed out the danger of disregarding the wider family groupings which characterise their social structure. In an address to a conference of tropical architects, Dr. O. H. Koenigsberger warned them:

> Social patterns in tropical countries differ widely from those in the West and unless the planner is aware of the differences he cannot hope to render useful service. This is illustrated most strikingly by the question of the unit of a household. In England the single family household forms the basis of all planning work. It is almost axiomatic for planning in the tropics to think in terms of multi-family households. Professor Holford has mentioned the experience of the Singapore Improvement Trust, where new single family units were split up into multi-family units almost as soon as they were built. This experience illustrates not only the almost insatiable demand for accommodation in Singapore, but also the fallacy of thinking in terms of single family households. A more detailed study of social traditions in Malaya and China would have resulted in the recognition of the fact that the unit of the household and the basis of residential planning in Singapore should be either a joint family or a single family with friends and boarders, or both combined.[1]

Most of the people I interviewed felt that the self-contained dwellings of the estate were designed to suit a European not an African way of life—or rather, European life as they had seen it amongst the expatriate officials in Lagos. As one man put it, 'A European house will have one big room, and another for a

[1] Proceedings of a conference on Tropical Architecture, March 1953, page 17. Dr. Koenigsberger uses 'household' in a sense which includes what I have called related households living under the same roof. In a comparative study of house design, G. A. Atkinson points out the value of a courtyard in tropical climates. See 'Mass Housing in Rapidly Developing Tropical Areas'.

bedroom, and a separate kitchen and pantry, and all with different kinds of amenities. And a man will just live there alone with his children. Even his steward's room will be far away at the back of the yard, and if he wants anything, he just presses a button. But we Africans don't live lonely like that. We call Europeans portmanteau people—with their portmanteau, they are ready to go anywhere.' The plan of the estate housing discounted, for the sake of a very English concern with privacy, the communal family life which flourished in the old courtyards of Lagos.

It is true that some of the residents at Suru Lere had found communal family life irksome: free at last from quarrels and interference, they relaxed in peace behind their suburban defences. But most family groups had split up regretfully, and they missed its warmth and companionship. It makes less work for everybody, since tasks can be shared, and there is always someone to look after children, or help in trouble. People feel secure amongst their kin, and the continual bustle of family affairs enlivens their everyday routine. And old people, particularly, may be neglected if they are isolated in separate accommodation, where they often cannot afford the rent and have no-one at hand to appeal to in difficulties.

This communal pattern of living requires for comfort a large, enclosed yard, where residents can cook, gossip, do their housework and even work at their trade. In a tropical climate, in dry weather, it is always more comfortable to be out of doors. The yard becomes the centre of the life of the house. The open space, especially if the roof projects over it, also makes it much easier to provide for visitors, since sleeping mats can be unrolled on the verandahs. Open hospitality is an obligation of Lagos social life, and the living space must be flexible enough to make visitors welcome.

At the same time, if a group of related households are to live together under one roof, they must each be able to reach their own rooms without continually intruding on the other's privacy. Relatives who shared a house on the estate often complained of overcrowding, though they had lived together contentedly before in as little space, largely because each house was planned as a single unit, one room opening off another. So if for instance two brothers, each with a wife and child, shared a two-roomed house, one of them had to pass through his brother's quarters whenever he went in or out. But in central Lagos, the rooms of the house are arranged along a common passage, or around the yard, each with independent access to the street.[1]

There seems no reason why houses for family groups, with a yard and rooms opening off them, could not be introduced as the rehousing estate expands. They are compatible with a reasonable standard of amenity: the L.E.D.B. has already successfully built freehold houses of a similar design. For the number of people they would house, they might be more economical in space and materials, and would suit many of the families much better than the present design. A courtyard house has a further advantage: if it is sited carefully, rooms can be added as a son grows up, and brings his wife home. Once families were thoroughly established on the estate, they might welcome the chance to buy their homes, and develop them in the traditional pattern of family life.

In this discussion of the rehousing estate, I have tried to suggest how all the aspects of social and economic life, which were contained within the streets of central Lagos, might be re-integrated as comprehensively within the new community. Without this, New Lagos will never recover the vitality of the old: it will only overburden the residents with a standard of living they lack the means to sustain.

THE PROBLEM OF SLUM CLEARANCE

The fundamental problem raised by the Lagos slum clearance scheme is this: how can a neighbourhood be physically destroyed, without destroying at the same time the livelihood and way of life of the people who have settled there? If these are disrupted, the clearance of slums is likely to do them more harm than good.

It seems that if compulsory rehousing is to be just, and a benefit to those rehoused, it must fulfil two conditions.

(1) The people must be able to afford it. In Africa, this must mean that it will cost them no more to live in their new houses than their old, since very few people have money enough to pay for

---

[1] In 1960, in order to complete their programme for independence, the L.E.D.B. were rehousing people at a density of 3·5 to a room, and hence more households had to share houses. There were complaints in the press. Later they adapted the three-roomed houses to provide separate entrances and kitchens, but the design was not readily adaptable for occupation by more than one household.

K

better housing. Those who can afford it and want to spend their money in this way will have already provided for themselves. If people are forced to pay for housing they cannot afford, their poverty will oblige them to restrict their participation in social life. Above all, it will withdraw them from their family, and this, in Africa especially, can cause great unhappiness.

(2) They must be able to re-establish their pattern of life in the new surroundings. They must not be too far distant from their kin, nor their work, and the same range of economic activities must be open to them. And their new homes must be so designed that they can be adapted to their way of life. That is to say, if they have depended for their livelihood on being at the centre of trade, they must be rehoused where they have the same chances of custom, or where there are alternative ways of earning a living open to them.

These two conditions are likely to be very difficult to fulfil in practice. The second condition can most easily be realised by rehousing the people on the site which has been cleared, but if they are to be less crowded than before, the buildings will have to be of several storeys. In Lagos, at least, this would have been very expensive indeed, and the cost could not have been recovered in rents. To rebuild in the suburbs, as in Lagos, brings down the cost of housing to government only to increase the cost in fares and living expenses to the people themselves, and makes it very much more difficult to prevent the disruption of family groups and economic relationships. New markets must be developed, new opportunities of employment provided; and the new estate must be able to absorb not only those removed from the slums, but relatives who wish to settle with them or near them.

Lastly, however the problem is tackled, it is likely to cost a lot of public money. The people to be rehoused may be expected to bear some of the cost themselves, on the grounds that they are, after all, enjoying a higher standard of housing, and the scheme is for their benefit. But many will not be able to afford to raise their standards, without sacrifices they would not make from choice. If their interests only are to be considered, it would be better not to rehouse them at all, but to use the available resources in a general improvement of health services and public amenities. The worst housing can meanwhile be gradually improved and rebuilt as national resources and personal incomes rise. But if, for reasons of prestige, neighbourhoods are re-developed to a standard in advance of the general growth of prosperity, the whole cost is a fair charge on the public purse. And the cost will include not only the buildings themselves, but substantial subsidies to the people who are to live in them.

This illustrates a dilemma which the newly independent nations of Africa will often have to face. They are urgently reaching out towards the prosperity of much richer countries, impatient of the limits set by their present wealth. For the time being, they have to make an uncomfortable choice: if they spread their resources evenly in overall development, the progress must fall disappointingly short of their aspirations. But if they attempt, here and there, to reach a standard not yet generally possible, they may overburden groups in their society with a standard of living beyond their power to sustain. In Lagos, it is beyond the means of the Federal Government to house the whole population to the standards of space and amenities that they would accept as minimal. That is not surprising, when even in London, Moscow and New York there are still congested and insanitary slums. But if one neighbourhood of Lagos is selected as a start, where standards will not be compromised, the people themselves cannot live up to them. Their way of life is suited to the social and economic pattern of Nigeria as it is, not as it may hope to be, and they do not earn enough to adapt themselves. The cost of unbalanced development is social disruption: even if rents are subsidised, economic opportunities restored at government expense, and compensation for hardship freely given, an artificial pattern of life is still being imposed. It is therefore doubly expensive to anticipate progress: not only does the selected project claim a disproportionate share of resources, it causes hardships which have to be put right by an expensive programme of rehabilitation. Only the elite can overleap the obstacles in the way of their country's development, and fine houses for Ministers, suburban estates for senior civil servants, hotels for diplomats, add an air of prosperity to Lagos which the occupants can afford to enjoy. But there is a danger, too, in allocating so much of the nation's resources to benefit the already rich. Unless these problems are understood, the symbols of progress will be achieved only at the price of growing injustice.

10

FAMILY LIFE
AND SOCIAL CHANGE

SINCE the physical space in which people live and work moulds their social behaviour, any radical rebuilding of a city calls into question the accustomed social pattern. The planner has to determine how far their present way of life satisfies—or ought to satisfy—the people he is to rehouse, and the people themselves are forced to revalue their traditions. They must either repudiate them, or reaffirm them by deliberate choice, perhaps in conflict with the ideal which leaders of society are seeking to impose. Slum clearance forces the pace at which society changes, and illustrates the pressures which are shaping its future.

The rehousing estate at Suru Lere was not designed to accommodate an existing pattern of life. It attempted to reform it, to retrieve human dignity from surroundings felt to be degrading. New standards of space and amenity, and a separate dwelling for each household, would encourage people to take pride in their homes, and adopt the accepted symbols of a progressive society. But in effect, if not intentionally, these reforms encouraged a much more radical change in social patterns. Well-spaced streets with shrubs and gardens could only be provided where the residents would be a long way from their work and their relatives, and they could only pay for this suburban life at the sacrifice of other claims upon their resources. Households became isolated from their wider family groups, and obligations to their kin were much more difficult to fulfil. The estate, therefore, encouraged a new interpretation of social values, in which privacy, independence and domestic comfort displaced traditional loyalties. These values were foreign to most of the residents of the estate, who were only frustrated by the difficulties which beset them when they tried to maintain their family ties, and the mutual exchange of gifts and services. But a minority welcomed their release from the traditional conception of family life more than any other advantage which the estate could offer. Such different reactions suggest that there may be a growing divergence in Lagos society, between those who still depend upon traditional family loyalties, and those who are increasingly frustrated by them: a divergence in styles of life related to a corresponding divergence in wealth and status.

Most of the householders interviewed, who resented the authority and interference of their families, and the continual demands upon their resources, were young men in relatively secure and well-paid jobs, with prospects of promotion. The remarks quoted at the beginning of Chapter 8 are nearly all from clerks under forty. This group in Lagos society tends to spend both their working life and much of their leisure in organisations inspired or promoted by European models. They work in banks, Government departments, foreign firms, and in their spare time they take an active part in the social betterment promoted and patronised by leading Lagos families. They are scouts, boys' club leaders, keen members of church clubs and societies for the prevention of cruelty to children and animals; they study first aid, attend British Council lectures, become special constables. They have constantly before them European conceptions of social responsibility and self-improvement. Positions of power are almost within their reach, and some of their schoolmates— with luck, ability and training—have already achieved them. They wrestle with correspondence courses far into the night, and dream of taking a degree abroad. Above them is the elite of senior civil servants and commercial managers who have inherited the villas, cars and four-figure salaries of the colonial regime.

This personal ambition is generally admired, and sanctioned by generous rewards for the most successful. Nigeria has inherited a sophisticated political and bureaucratic structure, and has begun to develop an equally sophisticated economy. Trained technicians and administrators are urgently needed, and there is no established aristocracy capable of filling all these posts. Education in the techniques of modern European culture is seen as fundamental to the progress of the nation, and is therefore the essential qualification for personal success. Nor is such education

confined to the children of the well-to-do: government scholarships, grants from tribal associations, the pooling of family
resources, promotion of talent by large commercial undertakings,
provide a chance for anyone with ability, and the luck to be in
the right place at the right time. Anything which frustrates the
exploitation of this talent is seen as an enemy of progress—
ties of sentiment which root people in a conservative way of life,
claims upon them which rob them of the rewards of personal
endeavour, deference to authority not based upon achievement.
Individualism and competitiveness have not been accepted in
mere imitation of European values. They are essential to bring
forward men and women competent to sustain the new structure
of political and economic power.

This conception of power as based on legitimate personal
ambition differs profoundly from traditional Yoruba culture.
For several centuries, the power and prosperity of the Yoruba
were not seriously challenged by any rivals. There was therefore
little incentive to evolve new political or economic techniques.
Nor was there much incentive to compete in private wealth;
fertile land was freely available for cultivation, and every one
was either farmer or craftsman, enjoying a very uniform standard
of life. Men could only compete in power. But opportunities to
seek power were carefully circumscribed. Unrestricted competition would only have led to civil strife, and the dominant per-
sonalities that would emerge from such conflict had no value in
a loose political structure where strong central government
served no purpose. Within the lineage, authority depended upon
seniority. Within the town, it lay with chiefs and societies of
titled men, who derived their positions from their membership
of lineages, in which a hereditary right to fill the chieftancy
rested.[1] The duties of the king himself were ceremonial and
sacred, rather than governmental, but he too was selected from a
particular lineage with hereditary rights. Rivalry for office was
therefore limited to a few candidates qualified by their membership of the appropriate lineage. But this principle was further
refined to prevent power from becoming entrenched in a

[1] In some towns, such as Ondo, chiefs also were appointed by the king irrespective
of lineage: but this was not general. For fuller descriptions of traditional Yoruba
government, see P. C. Lloyd, 'The Traditional Political System of the Yoruba', and
'Sacred Kingship and Government amongst the Yoruba'.

hereditary aristocracy. The lineages were sub-divided into branches, and each branch was entitled to fill the chieftancy in turn. The children of a chief were not eligible to succeed him: the privilege passed to a related descent group. Since these groups were large, eligibility for office remained widely dispersed. Nor could wealth become permantly concentrated in a few hands.

The holders of power might accumulate much personal riches in their lifetime, from the gifts presented to them in exercise of their office, but it was rapidly re-distributed. A man's personal property was divided equally between the groups of children born to him by each of his wives, and the share of each group was equitably sub-divided amongst themselves. Since a chief would have many wives and children, his wealth was therefore soon dispersed. The wealth acquired by the king himself while on the throne passed to his successor, not to his kin: it symbolised the standing of the kingdom, and he held it only in trust. Thus traditional Yoruba society discouraged competition for power, and limited its rewards. The farms on which the economy rested were in any case held in common by the family, and ultimately by the king on behalf of his people. No individual had a right to dispose of the use of land he had enjoyed in his lifetime. Both ownership and prestige lay in the lineage, rather than the individual, and no lineage could easily establish lasting ascendancy over the town.

In the nineteenth century, these political institutions came under increasing pressure. Invasion by Fulani emirates to the north, and the Kingdom of Dahomey to the west, could only be met by the strong central leadership which traditional forms of government tended to disarm. The city states began to break down in civil strife and internecine warfare. But before any new forms of political leadership had taken definite shape, the British had intervened. They did not at first introduce any great changes in the economy, and in accordance with a policy of indirect rule, tried to work through traditional forms of government as they understood them. The imperial government supported the conservative values of the culture. The challenge to their appropriateness came with the rise of nationalism.

This conflict of values between a conservative communalism and a progressive individualism is perhaps more evenly balanced in the West than in the North or East. Northern Nigeria is still a largely feudal society, in which the hereditary overlords have reasserted the legitimacy of their rule under the forms of political democracy. Most clerical and professional posts there have been held in the past by Southerners, and a Northern educated class is only now arising to test the compatibility of their traditions with a progressive society. By contrast, the Ibo had in the past a more democratic and individualistic conception of authority. Titles and membership of titled societies were open to any free man of good conduct who could pay the fees required for admission, and they were not generally inheritable. Though all important decisions were taken at public meetings, where every man in the community had a right to speak, the title holders dominated these debates. Even without a title, a wealthy man enjoyed considerable influence. A more individual control over land and property was possible than in Yoruba society. The culture was therefore always more tolerant of personal ambition, and ready to grant authority to those who achieved, rather than inherited, respect.

The predominant pattern of family life in central Lagos, however, derives from Yoruba culture. Although it has evolved further from its origins than in the Western Region, the moral and emotional pressures on the individual to subordinate his personal interests to those of his family group are still powerful. This subordination, which threatens a stultifying conservatism in political and economic life, still satisfies the need to belong, to express through the loyalty it demands a reciprocal commitment of affection. But it is increasingly difficult to reconcile the values inherent in this pattern of family relationships with those that influence clerks and professional workers in their career.

In the first place, age loses its authority when the experience of one generation becomes irrelevant to the next. In a rapidly changing society, children work at different occupations from their fathers, or the nature of the work has changed out of recognition. Amongst the men interviewed in central Lagos, only a quarter worked in the same class of occupation as their father, and on the rehousing estate only a fifth. The sons of farmers and traders became skilled craftsmen and office workers, and there was therefore much in which their fathers would not know how to advise or direct them. It is even more difficult to defer to seniority when children have more education and higher status than their parents. In formal family councils, the authority of age and education has sometimes been reconciled, by re-modelling their procedure on the lines of a committee, in which the best educated act as secretaries and treasurers. The family acts together less as a lineage under its head, and more as a voluntary society where kinship is the condition of membership. But in personal relationships, uncomfortable conflicts between educated ideals and traditional loyalties still arise. For instance, a grandmother has a recognised claim to keep some of her grand-children under her care, for company and to help her about the house. But an educated man may be reluctant to entrust his children's upbringing to his mother. She may not share his modern views on child welfare, may fill their minds with what he regards as superstitious nonsense, and treat their illnesses by old wives' remedies. Yet a refusal might deeply offend her. Again, a man who holds an executive position in a Government depart-ment or commercial firm must be ready to accept posting to branches and offices throughout the country in the interests of his job. But his parents may refuse to part from him. One man interviewed had had to give up a promising career as a commercial manager because his employers wished to transfer him to the Eastern Region. His father protested that it was too far—he was old, and unless he could see his son regularly, he would be very uneasy in his mind. The son resigned his appointment. Though he had not succeeded in finding another job with comparable pay or prospects, he still felt that he had done right. His talents had, however, been largely wasted. The conflict between educated ideals and legitimate ambition, on the one hand, and deference to the claims of affection on the other, can give rise to very difficult moral choices. Young men may early determine to assert their independence, so as to discourage their parents from making demands on them which it would be painful to refuse.

A similar conflict may arise over the place of a man's wife in his family. Under the traditional conception of marriage, a woman marries into her husband's family, and subordinates herself to their authority. Like her husband, she must accept the control and advice of her seniors, and share the life of the other women of her husband's compound. But the more educated the husband, the more likely that he will be influenced by Christian conceptions of equality and companionship in marriage. He sees them reflected in the social conventions of expatriate colleagues, and in the aims of voluntary and official welfare agencies. Moreover, the ideals of work as a vocation, and ambition as a social duty, encourage a mutual dependence of feeling in marriage which discounts other claims of affection. Just as the husband must be uninhibited by family ties if he is to pursue his career, so his wife must be free to follow him. In traditional society, marriage was designed above all to ensure that the lineage would continue to flourish from generation to generation. To the élite, it offers a relationship of mutual affection, which would make them less dependent for emotional security on the solidarity of the family group. As the authority of the lineage is called in question, so ʾs its claim to an overriding loyalty: people begin to search for ways of satisfying their need of love which can more easily be .econciled with the new structure of power.[1]

The family group does not, of course, intend to discourage the progress of its members. On the contrary, it will pool its resources to advance the most promising of them. The conflict arises when the men and women promoted by its efforts have to reconcile their obligation for this help with the demands of careers shaped by different values. The family does not act with disinterested generosity when it finances one of its members through university, since the graduate with his four-figure salary will be expected to contribute proportionately towards the needs of his kin. If they sell four houses to pay his college fees, and he returns from abroad to set himself apart, and spend his money on his home, they will feel cheated. But he is only following the cultural values he has acquired through his education, and which will earn him respect in his profession. The tradition of mutual support is the most concrete expression of family solidarity, but it becomes increasingly unworkable as the members of the family diverge in income and styles of life. As men are promoted in the ranks of the civil service or commercial firms, they find themselves no longer contributors towards a mutual exchange of gifts and services, but the victims of demands which may be beyond their means. To their poorer cousins, their

---

[1] A recent study of Ghanaian students describes very similar attitudes in a matrilineal society. See T. Peter Omari, 'Changing Attitudes of students in West African Society towards Marriage and Family Relationships.'

wealth seems so great as to be inexhaustible. Faced with insistent, even predatory claims, they may begin to restrict the range of relatives to whom they recognise an obligation. Many of them, besides, may have made their own way by government scholarships, or by promotion within their firm, and feel that they owe little to their kin. They themselves no longer stand to gain from the support of their relatives: they enjoy high and secure incomes, with a pension to provide for their retirement. Then, again, they are not altogether free to spend their money on others even if they wish. With the senior civil service post comes government quarters in a secluded suburb, designed for the commuter with his own car, and servants for his house and garden. The senior executive of a commercial firm will be expected to uphold its prestige in his social manners. To an employer, the claims of kin are a thoughtless exploitation of his executives which robs them of the rewards of their efforts. Whenever he tries to ensure them an income which would leave them free to concentrate without anxiety on their work, their financial liabilities only increase. Promotion may even put them seriously in debt, overburdened by new obligations they do not know how to refuse. Moreover, if men seek responsible positions in the interests of their family, rather than society as a whole, they are under pressure to abuse their authority by nepotism and corruption.

Salaried workers seem more exposed to this conflict of values than traders and independent craftsmen, who are not subject to the same expectations in pursuit of their livelihood. A man may become a wealthy trader without much formal education, and without moving amongst the professional élite. He can also better defend himself against over-reaching claims. Since only he knows his profits, he can fend off unreasonable demands by pleading a slump in business. And because his income is not assured, he may at some time need the support of his kin. The help he gives them is still a valuable insurance. A clerk, however, even if he is not in the most senior grade, has a good deal of financial security. His family are likely to demand relatively more of him, in proportion to his income. At the same time, he works in a hierarchy where his superiors enjoy an enviable standard of living, which he may try to imitate to uphold his self-respect. The extent to which people dissociate themselves from the moral, emotional and financial claims of their family group depends, therefore, on education, and the nature of their work, as well as their income.

Only the financially self-sufficient, however, can afford to be independent of their family group. The rest depend upon its support as their best insurance against hardship. They do not enjoy old age pensions, sickness or unemployment benefits, a guaranteed livelihood. Without the chance of a higher education, the opportunities in the civil service and managerial firms are remote. For them, the tradition of family loyalty still fulfils a vital need.[1]

So the patterns of life of rich and poor may increasingly diverge, as the most successful members of society detach themselves from their family group. And these differences could consolidate in a kind of class division which Nigeria has so far escaped. Family ties cut across hierarchies of status. A labourer can claim the hospitality and consideration of his senior civil service cousin. Wealth is redistributed in meeting family obligations, and the manners of an egalitarian society surmount gross inequalities of income. But the more the better-off are driven to restrict the range of their commitments, the less absolute will be the claim of kinship to override differences in income and status. Moreover, the present generation of managers and professional men has not arisen from an established aristocracy, and until the transfer of power and technical skill from expatriates to Nigerians is complete, there will be many opportunities for talent to enter the élite. The power and prestige of the successful represents a triumph over colonial dependence in which everyone can take pride, and those whose personal aspirations have been disappointed can still hope for their children. But in the next generation, the ranks of the élite will no longer be expanding so fast, and they may increasingly be filled by those whose parents have been able to buy them a higher education. Unlike

A senior civil servant to whom I showed a draft of this chapter commented, 'The pattern is changing along Western lines, and we have to adapt. Take my own case now, there are so many depend on me, and I'd much rather they didn't. And that goes for a lot of people. It tends to encourage laziness: people who know they will get so much from me, and be looked after—or at least not go hungry—it doesn't encourage enterprise. It follows that as the pace is getting faster, we must gear ourselves to the tempo. Many Nigerians think that. I mean people like myself, of course, not the "weaker". They would much rather have the status quo.'

traditional society, power rests on qualifications which a father can hand on to his son, and the most valuable economic asset is no longer land owned in common, but an education which by its nature cannot be shared. Poorer families will find it more and more difficult to promote their own candidates for the best paid jobs. Professional status will be less admired as a patriotic achievement, and more resented as the privilege of an exclusive class. For the excluded, their family solidarity may become generalised in a system of values which rejects outright an individualism whose rewards they cannot share. Modern technology and bureaucracy, therefore, continually widen the social distance which family loyalties have bridged. If this bridge collapses, there is no political tradition of egalitarianism in Nigeria powerful enough to challenge the growth of class divisions.

Thus the conflicts which the salaried workers of Lagos are trying to resolve in their family life involve a far-reaching reinterpretation of the values which their traditions express. The claims of the family group can be seen as an attempt to exert an outworn authority, inhibiting legitimate ambition; as an economic parasitism, robbing this ambition of its rewards; as an assertion of nepotism over social responsibility. But they also represent a system of social welfare; a challenge to self-seeking and class interest, a widespreading and secure emotional attachment. To abandon them would destroy the informal social justice and emotional security, which maintains the balance of a rapidly changing society.

Such a conflict of values is not peculiar to Nigeria, or even to African society. To escape an intolerable loneliness, people need relationships on which they can depend. But this unconditional support demands in return a commitment which limits their freedom, and the wider these relationships extend, the more people are rooted in a particular way of life. In a society which is rapidly changing, and especially in the groups within a society most exposed to change, the conflict becomes acute. As people respond to the opportunity to improve their wealth and status, they tend to become insecure: their feelings become restricted to the relationships which can adapt to their changing style of life, and the loyalties they have abandoned dog them with a sense of guilt. And the more society sanctions this individualism in the interests of its evolution, the more it becomes concerned with problems of isolation, neglect and social injustice. A wealthy nation can endeavour to restore at least the material imbalance by a comprehensive public welfare service. But Nigeria has neither the money nor the trained personnel to sustain such a service. It seems all the more essential, therefore, to adapt their traditions of family life, so that they may still provide emotional security and mutual welfare, and challenge the exclusiveness of wealth and status.

Such an adaptation may already be taking place in family councils. The procedure seems to be becoming more democratic, and more formal. It allows young men with education a voice in affairs, and the property which the family holds in common can be more efficiently handled. If, too, mutual welfare and the distribution of obligations are settled in these meetings, each member is better protected against exploitation. He can more easily refuse claims not sanctioned by the family council, and appeal to it against unreasonable demands. At the same time, he remains under a clearly formulated obligation to respond to the needs of his kin, to care for the old, and encourage the abilities of the young. The pattern of residence adapts itself correspondingly. The family house is no longer the home in which most of the members of the lineage live. It may be rented out, and the income used for the benefit of the family: or it may provide a home for dependent relatives. But it remains the headquarters of the family, a visible symbol of its unity and continuity. So, although each household may prefer an independent dwelling, where there is more privacy and less risk of quarrels between wives and their parents-in-law, they still have their roots in a common home. The traditions of family life need not merely disintegrate before the pressures of social change.

In this concluding chapter, I have tried to show how the conflict of values which confronts slum clearance is reflected in the evolution of family relationships. In both private life and public policy, the urgency of progress threatens the balance of society. In haste to command the symbols of material prosperity, an underlying disintegration may be dangerously ignored. If so, the next generation will inherit problems more intractable than economic growth and the assertion of nationhood. The experience of the Lagos Slum Clearance Scheme bears this warning out.

The plots on which had stood the homes of several hundred families remain unbuilt. But while their future is still being resolved, a few yards away has arisen the impressive façade of Nigeria's new Central Bank.

APPENDIX I

STATISTICAL SUMMARY

I. GENERAL CHARACTERISTICS OF THE SAMPLES

1. Marital State.

| | Central Lagos | | | | | | Rehousing Estate | | | Ebute Metta |
| | adults | | | householders | | | | | | |
	men	women	total	men	women	total	men	women	total	total
	%	%	%	%	%	%	%	%	%	%
Married	86	74	80	93	48	82	89	50	75	64
Single	10	2	6	5	—	4	2	5	3	32
Widowed	2	19	10	2	44	12	2	45	17	2
Divorced	2	5	4	—	8	2	7	—	5	2
Total %	100	100	100	100	100	100	100	100	100	100
Total No.	201	171	372	85	25	110	41	22	63	132

Notes:
(i) Married include those married by customary rites.

(ii) Widowed and divorced include only those not married at the time of interview, whose most recent husband or wife had died or been divorced from them. Divorce is here taken as any mutually recognised final separation.

(iii) The percentage of married in the first three columns of figures can be compared approximately with Ward A of Lagos township, which includes most of the slum clearance area. In the 1950 census 63% of men and 81% of women over twenty years of age are recorded as married. In Ward B, which includes the rest of the slum clearance area, the figure is 77% for both sexes.

(iv) Since there were only eleven women in the Ebute Metta sample, 64% married, the sexes have not been distinguished.

Statistical Summary

2. Age.

| | Central Lagos | | | | | | Rehousing Estate | | | Ebute Metta |
| | adults | | | householders | | | | | | |
	men	women	total	men	women	total	men	women	total	total
	%	%	%	%	%	%	%	%	%	%
under 30	18	28	22	23	16	22	24	9	19	60
30–39	27	27	27	18	12	17	47	18	36	28
40–49	26	19	23	36	24	33	24	14	21	6
50–59	13	13	13	12	16	13	5	27	13	4
60 or over	16	13	15	11	32	15	—	32	11	2
Total %	100	100	100	100	100	100	100	100	100	100
Total No.	201	171	372	85	25	110	41	22	63	132

Note: The age distribution of Ward A of Lagos township, 1950, from under thirty to sixty or over is 45%, 28%, 15%, 6%, 6%.

3. Length of residence in Lagos.

| | Central Lagos | | | | | | Rehousing Estate | | | Ebute Metta |
| | adults | | | householders | | | | | | |
	owners	tenants	total	owners	tenants	total	owners	tenants	total	total
	%	%	%	%	%	%	%	%	%	%
under 6 years	—	5	3	—	6	4	—	3	1	25
6–10	1	11	7	—	10	7	—	26	16	27
11–20	1	23	14	—	30	21	—	25	16	32
21–20	2	19	12	—	24	17	12	13	13	5
31–40	4	6	5	3	5	5	4	8	6	1
over 40	3	6	5	9	8	8	4	5	5	2
Born Lagos	89	30	54	88	17	38	80	20	43	8
Total %	100	100	100	100	100	100	100	100	100	100
Total No.	150	222	372	33	77	110	24	39	63	132

Notes: (i) Owners include relatives of owners, tenants those living with tenants.
(ii) Length of residence is calculated from the time of first taking up residence in the town.
(iii) The columns for owners and tenants on the rehousing estate refer to their status immediately before they were moved to the estate.
(iv) As there were only thirteen owners in the Ebute Metta sample, they have not been separately distinguished.

145

4. Length of residence in house.

| | Central Lagos | | | | | | Rehousing Estate | | | Ebute Metta |
| | adults | | | households | | | | | | |
	owners	tenants	total	owners	tenants	total	owners	tenants	total	total
	%	%	%	%	%	%	%	%	%	%
under 6 years	6	28	19	12	41	32	4	36	24	63
6–10	9	27	20	—	18	13	8	38	27	31
11–20	14	29	22	3	17	13	8	20	16	5
21–30	13	10	11	9	21	17	8	3	5	1
31–40	4	2	3	15	1	5	8	—	3	—
Over 40	5	1	3	3	1	2	8	—	3	—
Born there	49	3	22	58	1	18	56	3	22	—
Total %	100	100	100	100	100	100	100	100	100	100
Total No.	150	222	372	33	77	110	24	39	63	132

Notes: (i) Length of residence is calculated from the time of first taking up residence in the house.

(ii) The columns for the rehousing estate refer to the length of time they had lived in the house from which they were moved to the estate.

Statistical Summary

5. Birthplace.

	Central Lagos		Rehousing Estate	Ebute Metta
	adults	householders		
	%	%	%	%
Lagos	54	38	42	8
Western Nigeria	31	40	22	70
Eastern Nigeria	2	3	29	21
Northern Nigeria	12	16	2	—
Cameroons	—	—	—	1
Dahomey	—	2	2	—
Ghana	1	—	3	—
Elsewhere	—	1	—	—
Total %	100	100	100	100
Total No.	372	110	63	128

Notes: (i) Birthplace is not recorded for four of the Ebute Metta sample.
(ii) Western, Eastern and Northern Nigeria are defined by the present regional boundaries.
(iii) Of the total population of Ward A, Lagos township in 1950, 48% were born in Lagos, 34% in the West, 3% in the East, 11% in the North and 4% outside Nigeria. 37% of the population of the whole township were born in Lagos, and 38% in what is now the Western Region.

6. Ethnic grouping.

	Central Lagos householders	Rehousing Estate
	%	%
Yoruba	82	66
Ibo	3	19
Hausa	5	—
Others (Western Nigeria)	7	3
Others	3	12
Total %	100	100
Total No.	110	63

Note: in the 1952 Census, 91% of Ward 1 (formerly Ward A) were Yoruba, 73% of the total population of the township.

147

Statistical Summary

II. FAMILY RELATIONSHIPS

7. Household composition

	Central Lagos householders		Rehousing Estate	
	%	%	%	%
One generation:	19		24	
Person on their own		7		10
Person with other relatives or friends		4		2
Husband and wife (wives) only		6		6
Husband and wife (wives) with other relatives		2		6
Two generations:	68		61	
Parents and unmarried children only		39		24
Parents and unmarried children with other relatives		15		16
Mother with unmarried children only		5		9
Mother with unmarried children and other relatives		5		6
Mother with married children		2		3
Father with unmarried children		2		3
Three or four generations:	13		15	
Grandparents with married children and grandchildren		2		3
Grandmother with married children and (great) grandchildren		5		6
Grandmother with unmarried children and (great) grandchildren		3		6
Grandmother with (great) grandchildren		3		—
Total %	100		100	
Total No.	110		63	

Notes: (i) 'Other relatives' refers to others apart from parents and children in the head of the household's line.
   (ii) 'Married' children include widowed and divorced.
   (iii) Servants and apprentices living with the household have been excluded.

8. Number of adult relatives in the same dwelling.

	Central Lagos householders			Rehousing Estate
	owners	tenants	Total	
	%	%	%	%
0–2	15	72	54	78
3–5	9	27	23	17
6–10	34	1	10	5
11–15	12	—	4	—
16–20	30	—	9	—
Total %	100	100	100	100
Total No.	33	77	110	63

Statistical Summary

9. Proximity of Relatives.

Central Lagos % of householders with	same household	same house	Lagos island	Lagos mainland	outside Lagos	Total	Total No.
	%	%	%	%	%	%	
mother	6	10	28	10	46	100	63
father	—	3	14	14	69	100	29
nearest brother	14	15	25	9	37	100	81
nearest sister	2	7	28	17	46	100	71
nearest half brother	—	20	33	11	36	100	64
nearest half sister	2	5	28	21	44	100	61
nearest mother-in-law	1	—	37	13	49	100	70
nearest father-in-law	—	—	25	16	59	100	49
nearest brother-in-law	1	—	49	14	36	100	73
nearest sister-in-law	3	1	51	13	32	100	77
% of all brothers and sisters	3	10	26	13	48	100	285
children aged 16 or over	31	7	22	20	20	100	109

Central Lagos % of adults with	same household	same house	Lagos island	Lagos mainland	outside Lagos	Total	Total No.
	%	%	%	%	%	%	
mother	19	14	31	5	31	100	167
father	11	7	31	4	47	100	102
nearest brother	16	19	34	5	26	100	214
nearest sister	13	16	37	12	22	100	216
% of all brothers and sisters	10	20	32	10	28	100	693
children aged 16 or over	25	21	31	8	15	100	352

Notes: (i) The categories of distance are mutually exclusive.
(ii) 'Lagos Island' means the Western end of the island only, within a radius of a mile of those interviewed. 'Lagos mainland' includes the rest of the conurbation.
(iii) The totals of householders and adults exclude those without mother, father, etc. living.

Statistical Summary

Ebute Metta % of householders with	same household	same house	Lagos island	Lagos mainland	outside Lagos	Total	Total No.
	%	%	%	%	%	%	
mother	6	—	10	12	72	100	50
father	—	—	6	11	83	100	36
nearest brother	31	3	6	13	47	100	106
nearest sister	30	4	6	8	52	100	77

Notes: (i) 'Lagos mainland' here includes all the conurbation apart from the whole of Lagos Island.

(ii) Since the Ebute Metta householders are younger than the householders in central Lagos, many more of their brothers and sisters in the household are school children.

Rehousing Estate % of households with	same house	within a mile	Lagos island	elsewhere mainland	outside Lagos	Total	Total No.
	%	%	%	%	%	%	
mother	6	9	27	6	52	100	33
father	—	8	42	—	50	100	12
nearest brother	12	15	15	12	46	100	41
nearest sister	5	10	18	8	59	100	39
nearest half brother	12	19	24	12	33	100	42
nearest half sister	2	7	29	20	42	100	41
nearest mother-in-law	—	15	21	6	58	100	33
nearest father-in-law	—	14	29	4	53	100	21
nearest brother-in-law	—	3	28	13	56	100	39
nearest sister-in-law	7	8	23	11	51	100	35
% of all brothers and sisters	5	10	22	10	53	100	148
children aged 16 and over	43	5	9	13	30	100	63

Notes: (i) 'same household' is not here distinguished as a separate category, since nearly all relatives in the same house were in the same household as the subject interviewed.

10. Owners and tenants with relatives within a mile, central Lagos householders: see Table II, page 25 of text.

Statistical Summary

11. Frequency of contact with relatives.

Central Lagos % of householders seeing	daily	weekly	monthly	yearly	less often	Total	Total No.
	%	%	%	%	%	%	
mother	38	29	19	11	3	100	63
father	7	31	38	21	3	100	29
most seen brother	48	17	20	9	6	100	81
most seen sister	27	30	18	18	7	100	71
most seen half brother	38	31	14	14	3	100	64
most seen half sister	17	38	20	17	8	100	61
most seen mother-in-law	16	43	21	11	9	100	70
most seen father-in-law	8	41	25	20	6	100	49
most seen brother-in-law	15	44	14	15	12	100	73
most seen sister-in-law	14	42	19	17	8	100	77
% of all brothers and sisters seen	32	27	17	16	8	100	285
children aged 16 and over seen	58	21	14	4	3	100	109

Note: 'weekly' means one or more times a week, but not daily; 'monthly' one to three times a month but not weekly, etc.

The figures represent the average frequency of contact, derived from the number of days in the year on which relatives were seen. A person who regularly visited a relative every other year for a period has been recorded as visiting them for half that number of days annually—e.g. four weeks visit biannually is recorded as fourteen days a year—i.e. 'monthly' more than twelve but less than fifty-two days a year. The estimates are necessarily approximate: a person who normally saw a relative every day has been recorded as seeing them 'daily', even though there were occasionally short periods when he was away from home. In general, regular visits have been calculated according to their normal frequency: every day, once or twice a week, twice a month etc. Less frequent visits for several days or weeks at a time has been averaged on the basis of so many days a year.

Central Lagos % of adults who had seen	within a day	within a week	within a month	within a year	not within a year	Total	Total No.
	%	%	%	%	%	%	
mother	49	20	14	15	2	100	167
father	28	26	18	23	5	100	102
a brother most recently	50	24	11	12	3	100	214
a sister most recently	49	24	14	10	3	100	216
% of all brothers and sisters seen	44	23	15	13	5	100	693
children aged 16 and over seen	66	18	9	4	3	100	352

Statistical Summary

Rehousing Estate % of householders seeing	daily	weekly	monthly	yearly	less often	Total	Total No.
	%	%	%	%	%	%	
mother	21	24	28	12	15	100	33
father	8	50	8	17	17	100	12
most seen brother	29	29	5	15	22	100	41
most seen sister	18	20	26	18	18	100	39
most seen half brother	21	31	19	10	19	100	42
most seen half sister	7	29	29	15	20	100	41
most seen mother-in-law	6	27	30	25	12	100	33
most seen father-in-law	4	19	29	24	24	100	21
most seen brother-in-law	3	18	25	23	31	100	39
most seen sister-in-law	17	14	17	32	20	100	35
% of all brothers and sisters seen	17	23	23	11	26	100	148
Children aged 16 and over seen	46	21	11	8	14	100	63

See note to table of central Lagos householders.

12. Effect of where mother lives on contacts with brothers and sisters.

Central Lagos householders; % of brothers and sisters seen	Mother lives				Mother dead
	same house	Lagos island	Lagos mainland	elsewhere	
	%	%	%	%	%
daily	85	64	19	25	15
weekly	8	18	67	23	33
monthly	—	6	5	23	26
less often	7	12	9	29	26
Total %	100	100	100	100	100
Total No.	33	33	21	113	85

13. Contact with mother of men and women.

% of mothers seen	Central Lagos adults	
	Men	Women
	%	%
within a week	75	59
less recently	25	41
Total %	100	100
Total No.	93	74

Statistical Summary

14. Contacts with brothers and sisters by sex.

% of brothers or sisters seen	Central Lagos adults			
	Men		Women	
	brothers	sisters	brothers	sisters
	%	%	%	%
daily	48	45	39	45
weekly	22	28	19	24
monthly	10	15	20	15
yearly	16	10	16	9
less often	4	2	6	7
Total %	100	100	100	100
Total No.	221	168	147	157

15. Contact between parents and children by sex.

	Central Lagos adults					
	% of sons over 16 seen by			% of daughters over 16 seen by		
	men	women	both	men	women	both
	%	%	%	%	%	%
within day	67	79	72	60	57	59
less recently	33	21	28	40	43	41
Total %	100	100	100	100	100	100
Total No.	100	62	162	90	100	190

16. Contacts with brothers and sisters according to nearness of age.

Central Lagos householders

% of brothers and sisters	next in age to subject	not
	%	%
most often seen	62	43
not	38	57
Total %	100	100
Total No.	123	138

Notes: (i) Twenty-four brothers and sisters under age sixteen have been excluded. (ii) 'Next in age' includes all older and younger siblings aged sixteen or more, who immediately preceded or followed the subject interviewed in the order of their parents' surviving children. (iii) 'most often seen' includes all who were seen more often than, or as often as, any other sibling.

17. Contacts with brothers and sisters according to frequency of family meetings.

% of brothers and sisters seen	Central Lagos householders, where family met			
	weekly	monthly	yearly	not regularly
	%	%	%	%
daily	49	39	23	20
weekly	27	38	34	17
monthly	12	9	23	24
yearly	10	12	17	23
less often	2	2	3	16
Total %	100	100	100	100
Total No.	59	87	30	109

Note: 'monthly' = 1-3 times a month, 'yearly' = 1-11 times a year, regularly.

18. Contacts with brothers and sisters according to amount of help to relatives.

% of brothers and sisters seen	Central Lagos householders giving regular help to relatives	
	under £2 a month	£2 or more a month
	%	%
daily	26	40
weekly	23	32
monthly	17	17
yearly	25	6
less often	9	5
Total %	100	100
Total No.	158	127

Statistical Summary

19. Frequency of family meetings.

% of householders whose family met	Central Lagos	Rehousing Estate
	%	%
weekly	18	8
1 to 3 times a month	34	13
1 to 11 times a year	9	6
not regularly	39	73
Total %	100	100
Total No.	110	63

20. Attendance of family meetings.

Central Lagos householders	frequency of meeting			Alls meetings
average attendance	weekly	monthly	yearly	
	%	%	%	%
up to 10	17	15	10	15
11 to 20	44	29	20	33
21 to 30	28	27	20	26
over 30	11	29	50	26
Total %	100	100	100	100
Total No.	20	37	10	67

21. Family meetings of owners and tenants.

Central Lagos householders	Owners	Tenants	both
	%	%	%
Family met: weekly	9	22	18
1 to 3 times a month	67	19	34
1 to 11 times a year	9	9	9
not regularly	15	50	39
Total %	100	100	100
Total No.	33	77	110

22. Help to relatives.

% of householders paying monthly	Central Lagos			Rehousing Estate		
	men	women	both	men	women	both
	%	%	%	%	%	%
nothing	22	54	30	30	85	49
up to £1	17	13	16	25	10	20
£1 to £1 19s.	22	13	20	25	5	18
£2 to £3 19s.	14	8	12	10	—	6
£4 to £5 19s.	12	8	11	3	—	2
£6 or more	13	4	11	7	—	5
Total %	100	100	100	100	100	100
Total No.	85	25	110	41	22	63

Notes: (i) The figures represent the average monthly amounts paid to members of the family, excluding husbands, wives, unmarried children, and relatives in the same household.

(ii) Irregular gifts, contributions to family meetings or ceremonies and payments to meet emergencies have been excluded.

23. Relatives to whom help was given.

Number of central Lagos householders giving regular help

to grandparents' generation:
- grandmother   5
- grandfather   1
- great aunt   1

parents' generation:
- mother   43
- father   9
- aunts   9
- uncles   3
- father's wife   3
- wife's mother   3

own generation:
- brothers   11 } full or half siblings
- sisters   8 }
- cousins   3
- brother's wife   1

children's generation:
- nephews   3
- nieces   3
- married children   3

24. Relatives from whom help was received.

Number of central Lagos householders receiving regular help

from	fathers	3
	mothers	3
	aunts	1
	brothers	6 ⎫ full or half siblings
	sisters	3 ⎭
	cousins	1
	sons	8
	daughters	3
	grandchildren	2

25. Membership of societies.

% of householders belonging to	Central Lagos (100% = 110)	Rehousing Estate (100% = 63)
	%	%
religious groups or clubs	17	8
regional associations	30	41
friendly and mutual welfare societies	27	21
voluntary agencies	6	—
recreational clubs	8	8
any society	67	51

Note: 'Regional associations' means meetings of fellow-countrymen in Lagos from the same town or district.
'Voluntary agencies' include N.S.P.C.C., R.S.P.C.A. etc.

III. MARRIAGE

26. Form of marriage.

Number of current marriages contacted	Marriages of householders	
	Central Lagos	Rehousing Estate
by custom	118	49
in church	7	4
under the ordinance	1	2
Total	126	55

Statistical Summary

27. Number of wives according to religion.

% of married householders with	Central Lagos			Rehousing Estate		
	Christians	non-Christians	Total	Christians	non-Christians	Total
	%	%	%	%	%	%
one wife only	82	54	62	96	50	81
2 or more wives	18	46	38	4	50	19
Total %	100	100	100	100	100	100
Total No.	22	57	79	24	12	36

Note: Of the thirty in central Lagos with more than one wife, twenty-seven had two wives, one had three and two had four wives. Of the seven on the rehousing estate six had two wives and one had three wives.

28. Where wives live.

% of married men whose nearest wife lived	Central Lagos		Rehousing Estate
	adults	householders	
	%	%	%
with husband	92	89	86
within a mile	5	2	—
elsewhere Lagos	1	1	3
outside Lagos	2	8	11
Total %	100	100	100
Total No.	173	79	36

% of men with more than one wife whose furthest wife lived:	Central Lagos		Rehousing Estate
	adults	householders	
	%	%	%
with husband	62	47	57
within a mile	22	13	—
elsewhere Lagos	4	7	14
outside Lagos	12	33	29
Total %	100	100	100
Total No.	82	30	7

Statistical Summary

29. Where husbands live.

% of married women whose husband lived	Central Lagos		Rehousing Estate
	adults	householders	
	%	%	%
with wife	67	8	9
within a mile	19	33	—
elsewhere Lagos	6	18	36
outside Lagos	8	41	55
Total %	100	100	100
Total No.	126	12	11

Note: only the first column can be taken to represent married women in general, since married women who live with their husbands are not usually the head of the household.

30. Recency of contact between husbands and wives.

% of married householders who had last seen husband or a wife within	Central Lagos	Rehousing Estate
	%	%
a day	81	64
a week	2	9
a month	8	4
longer ago	9	23
Total %	100	100
Total No.	91	47

31. Visits away from home according to place of birth.

% of householders who had been away from home in the past 12 months	Central Lagos			Rehousing Estate		
	born Lagos	born elsewhere	Total	born Lagos	born elsewhere	Total
	%	%	%	%	%	%
for less than 2 weeks	73	45	56	82	72	76
2 weeks to 1 month	15	19	17	7	—	3
over 1 to 2 months	—	20	13	4	11	8
over 2 to 4 months	7	6	6	7	3	5
over 4 to 6 months	—	4	3	—	6	3
more than 6 months	5	6	5	—	8	5
Total %	100	100	100	100	100	100
Total No.	41	69	110	27	36	63

32. Wives' visits away from home.

% of wives of householders who had been away from home in the previous 12 months	Central Lagos	Rehousing Estate
	%	%
for less than 2 weeks	52	65
2 weeks to 1 month	21	11
over 1 to 2 months	7	8
over 2 to 4 months	12	11
over 4 to 6 months	7	5
over 6 months	1	—
Total %	100	100
Total No.	89	37
No. of wives not living with husband	25	7

33. Birthplace of husband and wife.

% of all current marriages where husband and wife are from:	Central Lagos householders	Rehousing Estate
	%	%
same birthplace and ethnic group	68	67
different birthplace, same ethnic group	30	20
different ethnic group	2	13
Total %	100	100
Total No.	124	55
Not known	2	—

Note: Among the couples of different ethnic origins on the rehousing estate, in one instance husband and wife were both born in Lagos: the other mixed marriages were all between people of different birthplace.

IV. CHILDREN

34. Who young children lived with.

% of householders' children under age 16 living with:	Central Lagos	Rehousing Estate
	%	%
both parents	55	45
mother not father	18	24
father not mother	7	12
grandparents not parent	12	15
other relatives only	7	3
non-relatives	1	1
Total %	100	100
Total No.	230	139

35. Young children in the household.

% of children under age 16 in the household living with:	Central Lagos	Rehousing Estate
	%	%
both parents	53	47
mother not father	15	19
father not mother	6	13
grandparents not parents	9	10
other relations only	12	9
non-relatives	5	2
Total %	100	100
Total No.	246	134

36. Young children of other relatives in the household.

% of relatives' children under age 16 who were related to the householder	Central Lagos householders		
	men	women	Total
	%	%	%
by blood	36	100	69
by marriage	64	—	31
Total %	100	100	100
Total No.	25	27	52

161

M

37. Where young children live.

% of children under age 16 living	Children of householders	
	Central Lagos	Rehousing Estate
	%	%
same house	69	69
within a mile	12	—
elsewhere Lagos	3	9
outside Lagos	16	22
Total %	100	100
Total No.	230	139

V. OCCUPATION, INCOME AND EXPENDITURE

38. Occupations of men.

	Central Lagos		Rehousing Estate	Ebute Metta	Lagos 1950
	adults	householders			
	%	%	%	%	%
Clerical workers	18	19	30	20	14
Skilled manual workers	29	32	47	32	32
Unskilled manual workers	13	16	12	14	19
Traders	26	15	7	15	9
Business owners and managers	4	12	2	3	1
Professional workers	1	1	—	3	6
Native doctors, herbalists, Arabic teachers	4	4	—	3	1
Farmers and fishermen	—	—	—	—	3
Soldiers, sailors, policemen	—	—	—	—	3
Students	—	—	—	—	2
Others	—	—	—	9	4
Not working	5	1	2	1	6
Total %	100	100	100	100	100
Total No.	201	85	41	121	75,126

Notes: (i) The distinction between business owners and traders is often difficult to draw: building contractors, importers and exporters and shopkeepers, have been classified as business owners rather than traders, but the difference is often only one of the amount of capital invested. There were no salaried commercial managers in the sample.

(ii) The final column is derived from the figures given for men aged twenty or over in the 1950 census: the categories are somewhat different from those used here, and have been re-interpreted.

39. Occupations of women.

	Central Lagos		Rehousing Estate	Lagos 1950
	adults	householders		
	%	%	%	%
Clerical workers	1	—	5	1
Skilled manual workers	2	20	14	5
Unskilled manual workers	—	4	—	1
Traders	87	64	63	48
Professional workers	1	4	—	1
Others	1	—	—	2
Not working	8	8	18	42
Total %	100	100	100	100
Total No.	171	25	22	58,492

Notes: (i) The final column is derived from the figures given for women aged twenty or over in the 1950 census.

(ii) The figures for the Ebute Metta sample are not given, since there were only eleven women interviewed.

40. Occupations of wives of heads of households living in the household.

	Central Lagos householders	Rehousing Estate
	%	%
Clerical workers	2	14
Skilled manual workers	6	5
Unskilled manual workers	1	—
Traders	82	38
Business owners	4	—
Professional workers	—	3
Not working	5	40
Total %	100	100
Total No.	86	37

Note: In the samples of adults in central Lagos, and householders in Ebute Metta, information was only recorded for the most senior wife, where there was more than one wife living with the husband interviewed. The figures for central Lagos include 78% traders and 15% not working, and for Ebute Metta, 55% traders and 32% not working.

M*

41. Proportions of workers self-employed and wage-earning.

% of householders	Central Lagos			Rehousing Estate		
	men	*women*	*all*	*men*	*women*	*all*
	%	%	%	%	%	%
self-employed	50	70	58	25	78	41
wage earning	50	30	42	75	22	59
Total %	100	100	100	100	100	100
Total No.	84	23	107	40	18	58

42. Incomes of men.

% earning a monthly average of	Central Lagos		Rehousing Estate	Ebute Metta
	adults	*householders*		
	%	%	%	%
0–£5	7	7	5	1
£6 –£10	29	26	39	30
£11–£20	37	36	39	46
£21–£30	13	19	5	12
£31–£40	7	2	10	2
£41+	5	9	2	2
not given	2	1	–	7
Total %	100	100	100	100
Total No.	201	85	41	121

Note: Income has been calculated from earnings, profits and rents. Where income varied from month to month, an average figure has been assessed. Gifts and allowances, regular or irregular, have been excluded.

43. Incomes of women.

% earning a monthly average of	Central Lagos		Rehousing Estate
	adults	householders	
	%	%	%
0 –£5	27	20	45
£6 –£10	33	28	23
£11–£20	21	40	9
£21–£30	6	4	5
£31–£40	5	4	—
£41+	2	4	—
not given	6	—	18
Total %	100	100	100
Total No.	171	25	22

Note: Income has been calculated as for the preceding table.

44. Incomes of wives of heads of households living in the household.

% earning a monthly average of	Central Lagos householders	Rehousing Estate
	%	%
no income	5	40
up to £5	44	35
£6 –£10	23	19
£11–£20	13	3
£21–£30	2	—
£31–£40	—	—
£41+	6	—
not given	7	3
Total %	100	100
Total No.	86	37

Note: Income has been calculated as for Table 41.

45. Average monthly incomes.

	Central Lagos householders	Rehousing Estate
Men	£23 19s.	£15 10s.
Clerical workers	£18 18s.	£18 19s.
Skilled manual workers (self-employed)	£17 16s.	£9 4s.
Skilled manual workers (employed)	£16 3s.	£15
Unskilled manual workers	£12 5s.	£9 8s.
Traders and business men	£51 10s.	£24 5s.
Women	£11 12s.	£2 19s.
Wives in household	£8 18s.	£2 5s.
All traders in household (including husband, wife and other relatives)	£11 12s.	£4 2s.

46. What traders sell: see Table VI of text.

47. Profits from trade according to kind of goods sold.

% of traders in central Lagos with average monthly profit of	Textile and cloth	Provisions and cigarettes	Foodstuffs	Other	All
	%	%	%	%	%
0 –£5	20	27	33	14	23
£6 –£10	25	38	36	23	30
£11–£20	27	27	17	37	27
£21–£30	18	5	10	3	9
£31+	10	3	4	23	11
Total %	100	100	100	100	100
Total No.	49	37	52	62	200

Note: The table is derived from the profits of the men and women traders interviewed in the sample of centre Lagos adults.

Statistical Summary

48. Where traders sell.

% of traders in central Lagos selling	
	%
at home only	51
at home and hawking	16
shop or stall	30
outside Lagos	3
Total %	100
Total No.	200

See note to preceding table

49. Average monthly expenditure on food and rent.

	Central Lagos	Rehousing Estate
Average monthly expenditure on food per household	£9	£8 6s.
Average monthly expenditure on food per household member	£1 17s.	£1 16s.
Average monthly rent per household (tenants only)	£2	£2 10s.
Average monthly rent per room	£1 16s. 7d.	£1 5s.

50. Expenditure as a proportion of monthly income (men only).

	Central Lagos	Rehousing Estate
	%	%
Average % of income of household head spent on food per month	52	56
Average % of income of household head spent on rent per month (tenants only)	14	18

Statistical Summary

51. Rent according to length of residence: central Lagos households.

% of tenant householders paying a monthly rent	Length of residence in house	
	0–10 years	11 years +
	%	%
under £2	38	65
£2 or more	62	35
Total %	100	100
Total No.	39	31

Note: Seven tenants not themselves paying the rent of their accomodation have been excluded.

52. Father's occupation: men householders only.

% of men householders whose fathers had been	Central Lagos	Rehousing Estate
	%	%
Clerical workers	11	17
Skilled manual workers	12	10
Unskilled manual workers	—	—
Traders	28	39
Business owners or managers	1	—
Professional workers	1	—
Native doctors, herbalists, etc.	6	—
Farmers and fishermen	29	34
Others	4	—
Not known	8	—
Total %	100	100
Total No.	85	41

53. Men following the same kind of occupation as their fathers.

% of men householders	Central Lagos	Rehousing Estate
	%	%
same class of occupation	24	20
not	76	80
Total %	100	100
Total No.	85	41

Note: The proportions are based on the same occupational categories as used in preceding tables.

APPENDIX II

Notes on the Methods of the Enquiry

1. THE SAMPLES OF HOUSEHOLDERS: CENTRAL LAGOS AND REHOUSING ESTATE.

(i) *Definitions*

A household was defined as a group of people living together under the same roof, who kept house together. In most cases, they shared the same meals, and their housekeeping expenses were shared. But where, for instance, the mother of the head of the household prepared her own meals separately, she was not treated as an independent household if she depended on an allowance from her son in the same house, and was in other respects part of the household. On the other hand, a wife who lived in a separate house from her husband was treated as a separate household, even though he provided for her, and she cooked his meals.

The head of the household was generally taken as the most senior member, unless they were living as a dependent of someone more junior. Among tenants, the head would usually be the man or woman who held the tenancy: among owners, the head would be the man or woman entitled by his family relationships to own or share the ownership of a house. For example, where a man had rented separate accommodation for his wife, and then placed his elderly mother under her care, the wife rather than the mother was taken to be the head of the household: had the old lady herself held the tenancy, she would have been the head. Again, in the one instance where a husband lived with his wife in a house belonging to her family, she was taken as the head: normally husbands were assumed to be the heads of their households.

The variety of circumstances is so great that the definitions of household and household head were evolved in the course of the enquiry, and I did not attempt to formulate them precisely.

169

Notes on the Methods of the Enquiry

(ii) The questions

The questions were grouped under the following heads:

Birthplace etc. Place of birth of head, and of husband or wives in the household. Place of birth of parents and husbands' or wives' parents. Length of residence in Lagos, and at present address. Length of residence at previous address in central Lagos for tenants on the rehousing estate.

Household. Age, sex and relationship to the head of other members of the household.

Housekeeping. Approximate monthly expenditure on food, drink and fuel. Amount and method of payment of house-keeping allowance, rent and light. Personal allowances to wives and children. Expenditure on clothes. Cost of fares. Distribution of housekeeping tasks. Where children go to school. How young children are looked after.

Occupation. Of all members of the household (except traders). Earnings of head and husband or wives. Hours of work.

Trade. Of all members of the household. Kind of goods sold. Where bought. Where sold. Average monthly profit. Former profit in central Lagos of traders on the rehousing estate. Amount of original capital, and from whom obtained.

Family. Whereabouts and frequency of contact with parents; full and half-brothers and sisters; husband or wives; children; grandchildren; parents and full brothers and sisters of husband or wives. Occupation of father, full brothers and unmarried sisters, adult children, husband or wife's parents and full brothers. Ages of husband, wives and children. Birth order of siblings. Relationship to other members of the family in the same dwelling. (All this information was recorded on a kinship chart.) Form of marriage. Amount of payment. Number of times divorced or separated. Frequency, size and subscription to family meeting.

Family help. Amount of regular and irregular help given to or received from members of the family apart from those in the same household, wives, husbands and unmarried children.

Social life. Membership of societies, subscription and frequency of attendance. Other leisure activities.

Religion. Faith. Frequency of church going.

Slum clearance. In central Lagos, attitude towards slum clearance, and future plans. On the rehousing estate, attitude towards removal to the estate and satisfaction with their present house. The handling of compensation received. Each interview lasted about one and a half hours.

(iii) *Recording and analysis*

The interviews were typed out from notes as soon as possible after they were completed, and a diagram drawn of their accommodation for the central Lagos householders. The information was later coded and punched on cards. Three sets of cards were prepared: for the head of the household interviewed, for each of his brothers and sisters, and for each of his children.

2. THE SAMPLE OF ADULTS, CENTRAL LAGOS

(i) *Method*

The team of nineteen interviewers were provided with instructions, which included general advice on interviewing, explanations and definitions of the questions, and an explanation of the purpose of the inquiry. After this had been fully discussed at a meeting, they did a few trial interviews. They were then provided with a list of names and addresses from the sample. Each interview was checked when returned, and if necessary the interviewer went back to the subject to correct ommissions and inconsistencies. Only those still living at the address listed were interviewed. The schedule of questions covered in a briefer and largely pre-coded form the topics of the interviews with household heads. The information was coded and punched on cards as for the samples of householders.

(ii) *Comparison of the central Lagos samples*

Since the two samples were chosen to represent different populations—one heads of households only, and the other all adults in the slum clearance area—the figures derived from them are not strictly comparable. The trend is the same, but particularly on questions of family relationships, the sample of adults appear to see more of their relatives, and live nearer to them. Since the larger sample is of individuals, not heads of households, it includes more women and young people. Nearly half the sample of adults are women, three quarters of them married, and over a quarter under thirty; while amongst the household heads women account for slightly less than a quarter, nearly half of them are widows, and only 16% under thirty. In both samples the great majority of men are married, but in the larger sample the proportion of bachelors is 10% as against 5% of household heads. The ages of the men distribute very similarly in both samples, and such differences as there are probably arise because so many people in Lagos can only estimate their age approximately.

But besides these differences in the composition of the samples, some of the discrepancies may have arisen from the inexperience of the interviewers used for the larger survey. The accuracy of their records are difficult to determine: the only independent figures against which to check them are those given in the 1950 census of Lagos. Compared with the census for the ward of the township in which they live, the ratio of men to women in the sample is the same, though the proportion of married men is rather higher, and of married women slightly less. For both sexes people under thirty are much under-represented, if the ages recorded in the census are accurate, and there are correspondingly more over fifty. Apart from age, the comparison suggests that the sample is representative of the population of the ward—which includes, however, areas outside the slum clearance area. For the clearance area itself, one further check is provided by the figures for owners and tenants derived from the L.E.D.B.'s census. In the sub-areas enumerated, the population of tenants varies between 60% and 70%: in all, 63% of men and women over sixteen years of age are tenants—3% more than in the large sample, and 7% less than in the sample of household heads. Both samples, therefore, accord very closely with the expected proportion of tenants. But since the accuracy of the larger sample is questionable, I have used its findings hesitantly, giving more weight to the most straightforward questions, and to the figures which agree best with the sample of household heads. Where the two samples contradict each other, I have drawn no conclusions. The census does not provide any data by which to test the representativeness of the samples of householders.

3. THE SAMPLE OF HOUSEHOLDERS, EBUTE METTA

This survey was carried out by my research assistant using the same schedule as for the sample of central Lagos adults, and coded like the other surveys.

APPENDIX III

LIST OF REFERENCES

ADAMS, CAPTAIN JOHN. *Observations on the Country extending from Cape Palmas to the River Congo.* London. G. and W. B. Whittaker, 1823.

ATKINSON, G. A. 'Mass Housing in Rapidly Developing Tropical Areas.' *The Town Planning Review*, Vol. XXXI, No. 2, July 1960.

BAUER, P. T. *West African Trade.* Cambridge, University Press, 1954.

BOWLBY, JOHN. *Child Care and the Growth of Love.* London, Pelican books, 1953.

BURNS, A. C., *History of Nigeria.* London, Allen and Unwin, 1929.

COMHAIRE-SYLVAIN, S. 'Le Travail des Femmes a Lagos, Nigeria', *Zaire*, February and May, 1951.

COKER, G. B. A. *Family Property amongst the Yoruba.* London, Sweet and Maxwell, 1958.

FORDE, DARYLL and JONES, G. I. *The Ibo and Ibibio-Speaking Peoples of South-Eastern Nigeria. Ethnographic Survey of Africa, Western Africa, Part III.* London, International African Institute, 1950.

FORDE, DARYLL. *The Yoruba-speaking Peoples of South-Western Nigeria, Ethnographic Survey of Africa, Western Africa, Part IV.* London, International African Institute, 1951.

IZZETT, ALISON, 'The Fears and Anxieties of Delinquent Yoruba Children', *Odu*, No. 1, January 1955.

LLOYD, P. C. 'The Traditional Political System of the Yoruba', *Southwestern Journal of Anthropology*, Vol. 10, No. 4, 1954.

LLOYD, P. C. 'The Yoruba Lineage', *Africa.* Vol. XXV, No. 3, July 1955.

LLOYD, P. C. 'Some Notes on the Yoruba Rules of Succession and on "Family Property".' *Journal of African Law*, Vol. 3, No. 1, Spring 1959.

LLOYD, P. C. 'Sacred Kingship and Government amongst the Yoruba', *Africa,* Vol. XXX, No. 3, July 1960.

LOSI, J. B. O. *History of Lagos,* Lagos, 1914.

OMARI, T. PETER. 'Changing Attitudes of Students in West African Society Towards Marriage and Family Relationships', *British Journal of Sociology*, Vol. XI, No. 3, September 1960.

SCHWAB, WILLIAM B. 'The Terminology of Kinship and Marriage among the Yoruba', *Africa,* Vol. XXVIII, No. 4, October 1958.

List of References

TALBOT, P. AMORY, *The Peoples of Southern Nigeria, Vol. I*, London, Oxford University Press, 1926.

WOOD, J. B. *Historical Notices of Lagos*. Lagos, 1877, 2nd Edition, 1933.

YOUNG, M. and WILLMOTT, P. *Family and Kinship in East London,* London, Routledge and Kegan Paul, 1957.

Annual Report of the Medical Services of the Federal Territory of Lagos for the Year 1957. Lagos, Federal Government Printer, 1958.

Annual Report of the Federal Medical Services 1958. Lagos, Federal Government Printer, 1960.

Economic Programme of the Government of the Federation of Nigeria 1955–60. Lagos, Federal Government Printer, 1956.

House of Representatives Debates. Session 1958–59, Vol. II. Lagos, Federal Government Printer.

Lagos Executive Development Board Annual Report and Accounts (1958–1959) Lagos, L.E.D.B.

Lagos Executive Development Board Annual Report and Accounts (1959–1960) Lagos, L.E.D.B.

Population Census of Lagos 1950. Lagos, Government Printer, 1951.

Population Census of the Western Region of Nigeria 1952, Bulletin No. 5, The Colony. Lagos, Government Statistician, 1953.

Proceedings of a Conference on Tropical Architecture, March 1953. Published by the Organising Committee, London, 1954.

Slums of Old Delhi. A Survey Report by Bharat Sevak Samaj, Delhi Pradesh. Delhi, Atma Ram and Sons, 1958.

INDEX

Abayomi, Sir Kofo, 10
Abeokuta, 24, 29
  marriage payments in, 45
Adams, Captain John, 4–5, 74n
Age; and contact with siblings, 153
  in sample interviewed, 145
  of men on rehousing estate, 100
Ajayi, L. G., xiv
Akinadewo, Samuel, xi, xiv
Akitoye, 7
Allowances, to wives, 78
Apapa, 1, 12, 96
Appa, 4
Ashipa, 3n
Aso ebi, 31
Associations; tribal, 39–41
  other, 41–42
  See also Societies
Atkinson, G. A., 127n
Awe, 24

Badagri, 4, 5, 7, 8, 72
Balogun, 2
Bauer, P. T., 76
Beecroft, Consul, 7
Benin, Kingdom of, 3
  conquers Lagos, 3
Birthplace, 147
  and absence from home, 159, 160
  of husbands and wives, 160
Bowlby, John, 64
'Brazilian' houses, 2, 6
Brothers and sisters; contacts according
    to where mother lives, 152
  contacts by family meetings, 154
  contacts by help to relatives, 154
  contacts by nearness in age, 153
  contacts by sex, 153
  frequency of contact on rehousing
    estate, 111–112
  proximity in central Lagos, 23, 25
  proximity on rehousing estate,
    109–110
  united through mother, 30
  See also half brothers and sisters
Brothers- and sisters-in-law, proximity
    in central Lagos, 25
Building; regulations for plots in
    central Lagos, 87
  costs, 87
Burns, A. C., 3n

Burton, Sir Richard, 8
Businessmen; defined, 68n
  incomes of, 71

Capital, for wife's trade, 53
  and trading patterns, 76–77
Carter Bridge, vii, 1
Central Lagos; choice as slum clearance
    area, 118–119
  described, 22–23
  expenditure in, 77–81
  rents in, 79–80
  replanning of, 119–123
  riot in, 87–88
  samples in, 169, 171–172
Children; care of, 161
  contribution to housekeeping by, 80
  delinquency of, 57n, 62
  discipline of, 59–60
  frequency of contact on housing
    estate, 111–112
  in household, 161
  not living with parents, 56–59
  proximity in central Lagos, 23, 25
  proximity on rehousing estate, 109–110
  where living, 56, 57, 62
Christians; attitude to polygamy of, 48
  proportion of on rehousing estate, 100
Christmas, 61
Class divisions, and family loyalties,
    140–141
Clerks; incomes of, 71
  influenced by European values, 133
  proportion of on rehousing estate, 100
Cloth, *see* textiles
Clothes, expenditure on, 78–79
Coker, G. B. A., 3n, 20n
Comhaire-Sylvain, S., 76n
Companionship, in marriage, 54–55,
    137–138
Compensation, 85, 86–87, 89, 120,
    121–122
  division of, 91–92
Contacts, with relatives, 110–112,
    151–154
  See also, Children, Fathers, Husbands
    and Wives, Mothers, Parents
Cost of living; in central Lagos, 78
  on rehousing estate, 102–105
  See also, Allowances, Clothes, Food,
    Housekeeping, Incomes

175

Index

178

Index

Questionnaire, xiii
Questions, asked at interviews, 170

Railway, construction of, 9
Re-allocation of plots in central Lagos, 85, 86–87
Redevelopment charges, 85, 86–87
Refusal, rate of, xiii
Rehousing, LEDB's responsibility for, 85
Rehousing estate; as expression of social values, 132
attitude of residents towards, 100, 102
attraction of, 97–100
avoidance of, 100–101
described, 96–97
family relationships on, 109–115
future development of, 123–129
language of interviews in, xiv
malaria, in, 118
provision of markets on, 125
purpose of, 85
samples in, xi–xii, 169
Relatives; care of children by, 56, 58–59
children of in household, 161
frequency of contact, 151–152
frequency of contact on rehousing estate, 110–112
helped, 36–39, 154, 156
helping, 157
in same dwelling, 128–129, 148
proximity of, 149–150
proximity of in central Lagos, 23–26
proximity of in Ebute Metta, 26–27
proximity of on rehousing estate, 109–110
visiting between, 28–31
Relatives by marriage; contacts with, 111
proximity of, 109
Religion, and number of wives, 158
Rent; according to length of residence, 168
as proportion of income, 167
average, 167
expenditure on, 79–80
in central Lagos, 79–80
on rehousing estate, 102–103
Repatriated slaves, 6, 9
Residence, length of, *see* Length of Residence
Resident's Association, central Lagos, 86, 88
Chairman of, *see* Ajaya, L. G.
Riot, in central Lagos, 87–88

Rooms; density of occupation, 82, 129n
in rehousing estate houses, 97

Samples; compared, 171–172
described, xi–xiii
of adults, 171
of householders, 169
sizes of, xiii
Sampling, problems of, xiv–xv
Schwab, William B., 14n
Self-employed; in central Lagos, 69
on rehousing estate, 107
proportion of, 164
Seniority; amongst wives, 49
and attendance at family meetings, 34
and education, 136–137
as determinant of status, 14–15
Servants, 62–63
Sewage scheme, 117–118
Sexual relations, barred during pregnancy and nursing, 48
Sharing of houses, 128–129
Shomolu, 100
Siblings, *see* Brothers and Sisters
Singapore Improvement Trust, 127
Sisters, sisters-in-law, half sisters, *see* Brothers, Brothers-in-law, Half brothers
Slave trade; extent, 4
of Lagos, 5–6
suppression of, 6–7
Slum clearance; attitude in central Lagos towards, 90–95
effect on cost of living, 102–105
effect on family relationships, 109–115
effect on marriage, 113–114
effect on old people, 92
effect on trade, 105–108
fundamental problems of, 129–131
influence on social change, ix, 132
justifications of, 117–119
Slum Clearance Area; described, vii–viii
language of interviews in, xiv
population of, xiii
sample of adults in, xii
sample of households in, xii
Slum Clearance Scheme, ix
and standards of hygiene, 83
cost of compensation for, 89
protests against, 86–89
provisions of, 85
scope of, 84
Social Welfare Department, 45, 64

179

Index

Societies, membership of, 157
  on rehousing estate, 105, 113
  See also, Associations
Son, responsibilities of eldest, 36–37
Specialization in trade, of men and
  women, 73–75
Statistics, Federal Department of, 79
Stepmother, child's fear of, 57n
Subscriptions, 33, 34, 35, 40, 41, 42
Suru Lere, 85, 96
  markets in, 125
  See also, Rehousing estate, Industry

Taiwo, Chief, 2
Talbot, P. Amoury, 3n
Tenants; attitude towards slum clearance, 93–94
  family meetings of, 155
  frequency of family meetings of,
    35–36
  in central Lagos, birthplace of, 24
  in central Lagos, eviction of, 20–21
  in central Lagos, family relationships
    of, 24–25
  in central Lagos, length of residence
    of, 24–25
  in central Lagos, percentage of resi-
    dents, 20
  in central Lagos, proportions, 172
  proportion in Ebute Metta, 26
  provision for in redevelopment, 122
Textiles, trade in, 73–74
Tinubu, Madame, 2
Town Council, Lagos, 125
Trade; affected by slum clearance,
  93–94, 105–108
  dependence on concentration,
    124–125
  pattern in central Lagos, 72–77
  profits of, 167
Traders; dependence on central loca-
  tion, 71
  earnings on rehousing estate, 107–108
  incomes of, 71
  proportion in central Lagos, 67
  provision for in redevelopment, 122
  where selling, 167
Trading; of wives, 53–54
  restrictions, 126
Transport, cost on rehousing estate,
  103–104, 124
  See also, Journey to Work
Treaty; Akitoye's, 7

Treaty; Dosunmu's, 8

Visiting; between relatives, 28–31
  expense of, 29–30

Wage earners; proportion, 164
  proportion on rehousing estate, 100
Wares sold by traders, 75
Weddings, cost of, 45–47
Western Avenue, 96
Western Region of Nigeria, Lagos
  boundary with, 1
White cap chiefs, 3
Wida, 4
Widow inheritance, 15, 52
Willmott, Peter, ixn
Wives; allowances to, 78
  earnings in central Lagos, 71
  earnings on rehousing estate, 108
  economic independence of, 52–54, 64,
    65
  help to husbands, 53–54, 80–81
  incomes of, 165
  living apart from husbands, 51–52,
    114
  number according to religion, 158
  occupations of, 163
  position in husband's family, 137–138
  time spent away from home, 51, 160
  where living, 158
Women; attitude towards polygamy,
  49–50
  earnings in central Lagos, 71
  earnings on rehousing estate, 107–108
  incomes of, 165
  occupations of, 163
  position in husband's lineage, 15
  position in own lineage, 16
  proportion not working, 67–68
Wood, J. B., 3n
Workers' estate, 96, 102–103

Yaba, xiii, 1, 12
Yards, use of, 128
Yoruba; associations, 41
  betrothal customs, 43n
  kinship terms, 14–15
  political structure of, 134–135
  proportion of Lagos population, 12
  proportion in samples, 147
  traditional family structure, 12–16
Yoruba language, interviews in, xiv
Yoruba states, civil war in, 9
Young, Michael, ixn